Physical Memory Analysis

Fundamentals

Anniversary Edition

Dmitry Vostokov
Software Diagnostics Services

Published by OpenTask, Republic of Ireland

OpenTask books are available through booksellers and distributors worldwide. For further information or comments, send requests to press@opentask.com.

A CIP catalog record for this book is available from the British Library.

ISBN-l3: 978-1912636808 (Paperback)

First printing, 2014
Revision 2 (July 2015)
Revision 3 (June 2020)

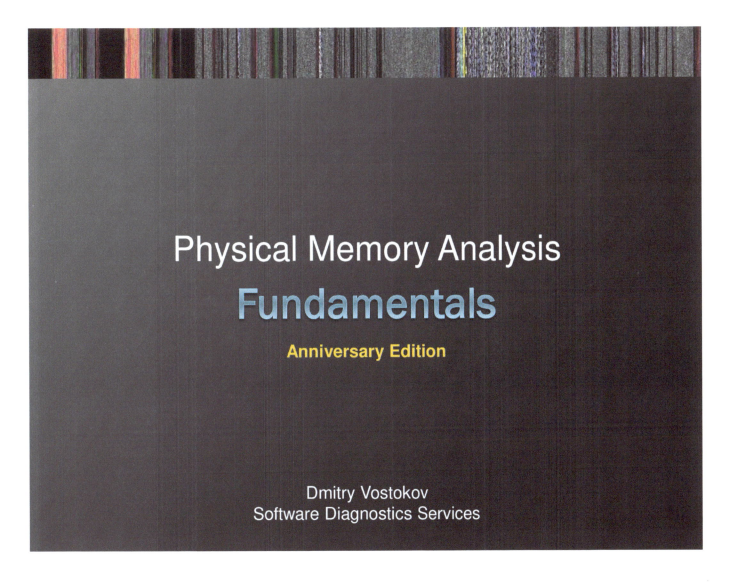

Hello, everyone! More than six years have been passed since I presented the third version of the Complete Crash and Hang Memory Dump Analysis webinar (renamed to Fundamentals of Physical Memory Analysis) and almost 10 years since its first version. Before that time, I found this topic a bit neglected, so I had decided to summarize it and make a presentation. Many new memory dump analysis patterns have been identified since that time, and new training courses became available, so I decided to make an anniversary edition. Slides and their transcript text have been significantly revised, links and references have been checked and updated, and the whole WinDbg analysis session has been redone for Windows 10.

Facebook:
http://www.facebook.com/SoftwareDiagnosticsServices

LinkedIn:
http://www.linkedin.com/company/software-diagnostics-services

Twitter:
http://twitter.com/DumpAnalysis

Prerequisites

To Be Discussed Later

We use these boxes to introduce useful vocabulary to be discussed in later slides

Working knowledge of:

- WinDbg (installation, symbols)

- Basic user process dump analysis

- Basic kernel memory dump analysis

Physical memory analysis is a big topic. I assume that you already know what kernel, process, physical, and virtual memory spaces are, how to set up and use symbols files, basic WinDbg commands to get stack traces, list loaded modules, and display module information.

Agenda (Summary)

- ⊙ Basics

- ⊙ Patterns

- ⊙ Exercise

- ⊙ Guide

First, I remind you and discuss the fundamental concepts of what a physical memory space is and how it relates to what we see in WinDbg debugger when we open a complete memory dump. Then I discuss a pattern language to communicate memory dump analysis findings. Next, I do a quick hands-on demonstration and finally provide a short, incomplete guide. You can type your questions, and I do my best to answer them either at the end of the Webinar or publish them later on a dedicated page for this revision.

Agenda (Basics)

- ◉ Dump generation

- ◉ Memory spaces

- ◉ Major challenges

- ◉ Common commands

Here I talk about the need for complete or physical memory dumps and how to force them; the differences between various memory spaces; the challenges we face when we start looking at physical memory and common WinDbg commands essential to know.

Platform: Windows

The pattern-oriented approach is applicable to other OS through different memory analysis pattern implementations

Note: we do not discuss BSOD crashes here as most of the time kernel memory dumps are sufficient for analysis

In this presentation, I cover only Windows desktop and server platforms. But the pattern-oriented approach can be reused for other platforms.

Memory Analysis

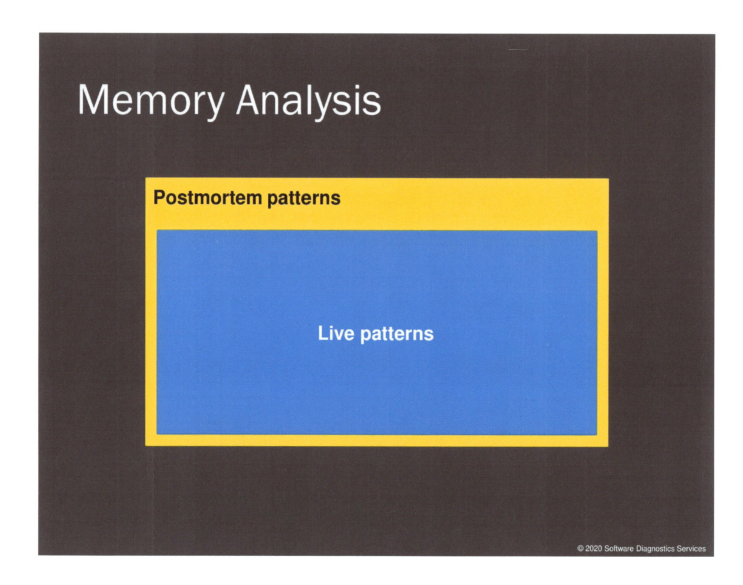

Postmortem patterns

Live patterns

Physical memory analysis can be live, for example, during a debugging session, or it can be postmortem via memory dumps. The same catalog of memory analysis patterns is used. For example, a memory leak can be diagnosed on a live system by examining memory at different times. In the case of postmortem memory dump analysis, we need a set of consecutive memory dumps saved after some interval. However, in the case of live analysis, some patterns may not be available such as related to memory dump specifics.

Dump Configuration

To Be Discussed Later
Truncated Dump pattern
Manual Dump pattern

- Control Panel \ System and Security \ System \ Advanced system settings \ Advanced \ Start-up and Recovery
- Page file size should be greater than the amount of physical memory by a few MB
- Configuration for Server Core, small system partitions, or virtual disk systems

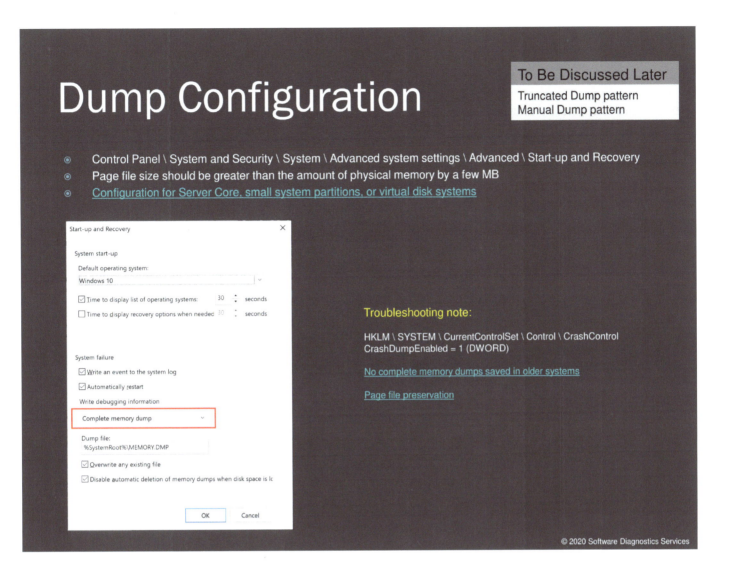

Troubleshooting note:

HKLM \ SYSTEM \ CurrentControlSet \ Control \ CrashControl
CrashDumpEnabled = 1 (DWORD)

No complete memory dumps saved in older systems

Page file preservation

© 2020 Software Diagnostics Services

Why do we need complete memory dumps? Suppose we have an incident when a system doesn't respond to a user, program, or network requests (appears to hang) or very sluggish for users (long delays). We can get a kernel memory dump to check for various patterns such as spikes in kernel mode, kernel pool leaks, insufficient physical memory (extensive paging), resource contention, or deadlocks between executive resources (famous **!locks** command). However, we might not find all of that. We would need to look at processes to find out the following: any blocked GUI threads, wait chains between processes, deadlocks in user-mode synchronization mechanisms such as critical sections, process heap corruption, spikes in user mode, and error message boxes. In summary, we would need to look at process spaces that are missing in kernel memory dumps. Other typical scenarios occur in server environments like user session freeze or connection denied messages. Sometimes it is the only option available when we want to examine a live system offline.

Configuration for Server Core, small system partitions, or virtual disk systems:

https://docs.microsoft.com/en-us/windows-server/administration/server-core/server-core-memory-dump

No complete memory dumps saved in older systems:

https://docs.microsoft.com/en-us/archive/blogs/wer/kernel-dump-storage-and-clean-up-behavior-in-windows-7

Page file preservation:

https://docs.microsoft.com/en-us/windows-hardware/drivers/debugger/cab-files-that-contain-paging-files-along-with-a-memory-dump

Dump and Memory Acquisition

- General

- Killing a system process like csrss.exe (-W8.1)

- LiveKd (options for more consistency)

- Live debugging (.dump)

- Memory forensic tools

There are many methods to force a physical memory dump from a live system. Some methods freeze all CPUs except the one that is currently saving memory directly to a page file bypassing file systems. This ensures memory dump consistency. Live methods, therefore, may save a non-consistent memory dumps as parts to be saved may change pointers to the first parts already saved. In Memory Dump Analysis Anthology, Volume 3, I outlined a method called OSMOSIS, that copies compressed memory to a separate reserved memory region and then saves the latter as a consistent memory dump.

The latest versions of the Windows Sysinternals LiveKd tool provide options for consistency. You can also find 3rd-party tools for memory acquisition.

General:
https://docs.microsoft.com/en-us/windows/client-management/generate-kernel-or-complete-crash-dump

LiveKd:
https://docs.microsoft.com/en-gb/sysinternals/downloads/livekd

Physical Memory

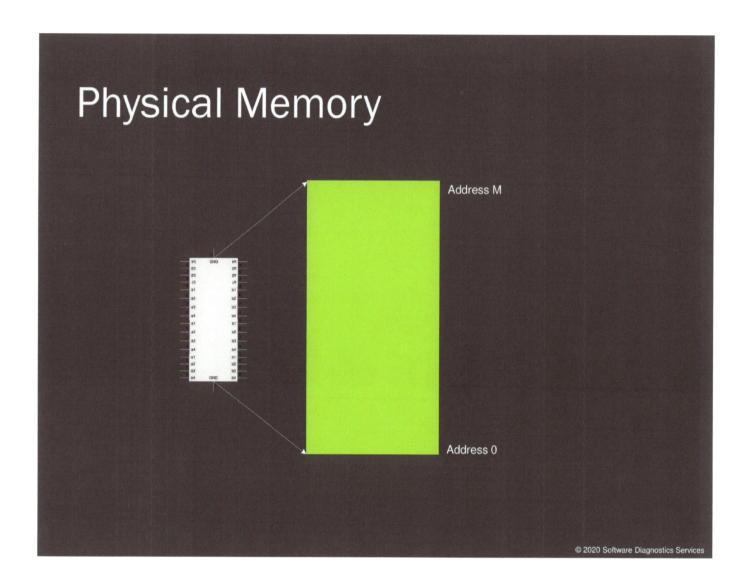

Before we look at a debugger's view of physical memory, we recall a few definitions. Physical memory space is just a linear ordering of physical memory cells.

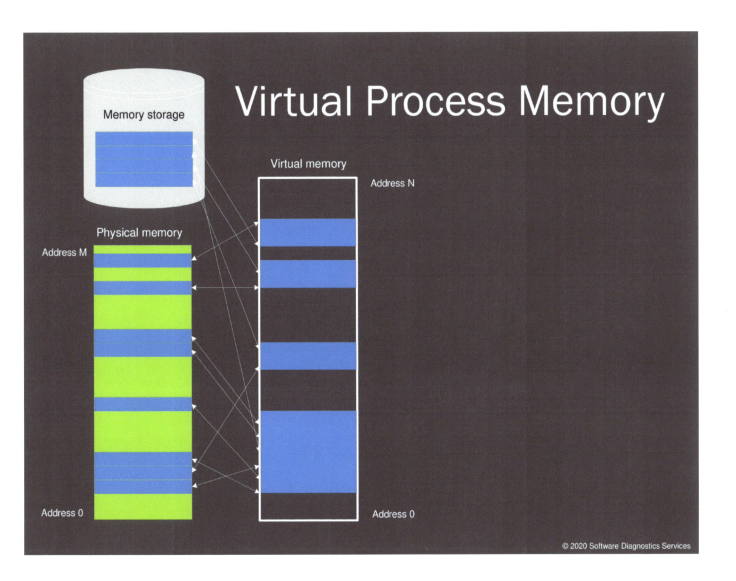

Virtual process memory is how a process sees its memory during execution and how we see it in a debugger. Process pages can be randomly distributed in physical memory, and even some can be located in a page file. However, when we break into a debugger on a live system or open a complete memory dump, we see a linear ordering of memory cells that comprise a current process memory. The debugger takes care of this physical to virtual address space mapping.

Memory Spaces

- Complete memory == Physical memory
- We always see the current virtual process space
- Kernel space is the same

To Be Discussed Later

WinDbg command to switch to a different process context:

.process

Kernel Space

Context switch

User Space

current process A
(taskmgr.exe)

Kernel Space

User Space

current process B
(svchost.exe)

© 2020 Software Diagnostics Services

So, when we open a complete physical memory dump, we see the virtual space of the current process (called the current process context). We need to be aware of the current process. When we switch to another process, we need to make sure that the debugger switched to the appropriate physical to virtual space mapping and reloaded symbols for user space modules. Kernel space always stays the same.

Major Challenges

To Be Discussed Later

WinDbg extension command
to dump all stack traces:

!process 0 3f

- Vast memory space to search
- Multiple processes (user spaces) to examine
- User space view needs to be correct when we examine another thread
- Large file size (x64)

User Space

The simple approach for blue screen crash dumps to check their problem thread stack traces is no longer applicable here. Even checking a few processes of interest is not enough because we might miss something. All challenges are obvious except the 3rd one about examining threads. Because threads belong to processes when we examine them, we need to make sure we also have correct process context: physical to virtual memory mapping and correct symbols for user space are loaded.

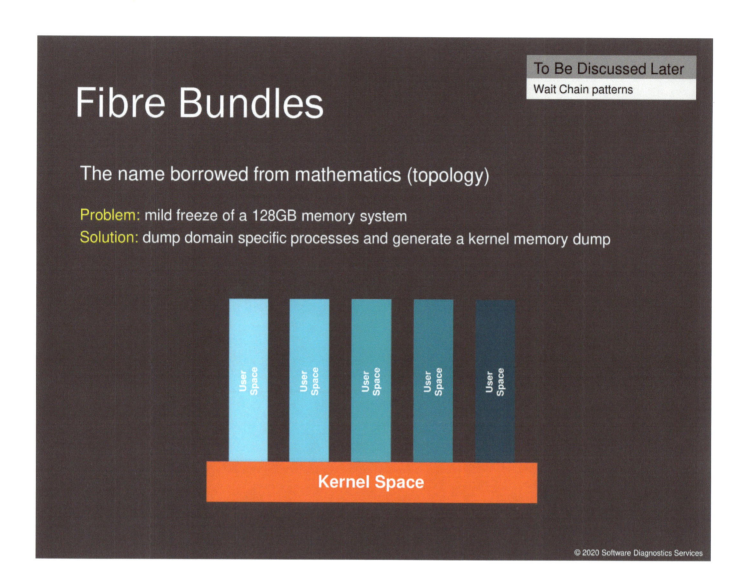

In the case of physical memory, there exists another alternative. The fiber bundle is a memory space that consists of kernel space and individual process virtual address spaces. A "complete" dump of physical memory might miss some pages residing in a page file. But a fiber bundle set of memory dumps is more "complete" because missing pages of process memory are brought from the page file when we dump individual processes. What we lose here is a synchronicity that could make some memory references inconsistent because kernel and process memory dumps are generated at different times.

Common Commands

- **.logopen <file>**
  Opens a log file to save all subsequent output

- **View commands**
  Dump everything or selected processes and threads (context changes automatically)

- **Switch commands**
  Switch to a specific process or thread for a fine-grain analysis

Because the output of commands is very lengthy most of the time, it is useful to open a log file and later analyze its content as text. To save time, we can include many commands in a script. Such scripts are also useful for secure environments if you don't want to send a memory dump but prefer to extract textual information and send it to 3rd-party technical support.

View Commands

- **!process 0 3f**
  Lists all processes (including times, environment, modules) and their thread stack traces

- **!process 0 1f**
  The same as the previous command but without PEB information (more secure)

- **!process <address> 3f or !process <address> 1f**
  The same as the previous commands but only for an individual process

- **!thread <address> 1f**
  Shows thread information and stack trace

- **!thread <address> 16**
  The same as the previous command but shows the first 3 parameters for every function

These are different commands to view an individual process and its threads, and all processes and threads with automatic process context change and symbols reload.

Switch Commands

To Be Discussed Later

x86 stack trace from WOW64 process:

.thread /w

◉ **.process /r /p <address>**

Switches to a specified process. Its context becomes current. Reloads symbol files for user space. Now we can use commands like !cs

```
0: kd> .process /r /p fffffa80044d8b30
Implicit process is now fffffa80`044d8b30
Loading User Symbols
. . . . . . . . . . . . . . . . . . . . . . . . . . . . . . .
```

◉ **.thread <address>**

Switches to a specified thread. Assumes the current process context
Now we can use commands like k*

◉ **.thread /r /p <address>**

The same as the previous command but makes the thread process context current and reloads symbol files for user space:

```
0: kd> .thread /r /p fffffa80051b7060
Implicit thread is now fffffa80`051b7060
Implicit process is now fffffa80`044d8b30
Loading User Symbols
. . . . . . . . . . . . . . . . . . . . . . . . . . . . . . .
```

© 2020 Software Diagnostics Services

After we check the command output or the contents of a log file, we might need to manually switch to a particular process context or thread when we find something suspicious and want to investigate further.

Agenda (Patterns)

- ⊙ Pattern-oriented analysis

- ⊙ Pattern classification

- ⊙ Pattern examples

- ⊙ Common mistakes

Now I briefly talk about patterns.

Pattern-Oriented Diagnostic Analysis

Diagnostic Pattern: a common recurrent identifiable problem together with a set of recommendations and possible solutions to apply in a specific context.

Diagnostic Problem: a set of indicators (symptoms, signs) describing a problem.

Diagnostic Analysis Pattern: a common recurrent analysis technique and method of diagnostic pattern identification in a specific context.

Diagnostics Pattern Language: common names of diagnostic and diagnostic analysis patterns. The same language for any operating system: Windows, Mac OS X, Linux, ...

Checklist: http://www.dumpanalysis.org/windows-memory-analysis-checklist

Patterns: http://www.dumpanalysis.org/blog/index.php/crash-dump-analysis-patterns/

Typical pattern example: we identified process heap corruption and suggested instrumentation to narrow down a set of suspicious modules by using either *gflags.exe* from Debugging Tools for Windows or Application Verifier.

Pattern Classes

- ◉ Blocked threads

- ◉ Wait chains

- ◉ Resource consumption

- ◉ Corruption signs

- ◉ Special processes

In this slide, you see a few pattern classes. An example of a blocked thread could be a print spooler that attempted a print driver setup presenting a dialog box, or some service loaded module showing an error message box. Wait chains can include threads waiting for critical sections or executive resources, or involving interprocess communication mechanisms such as remote and local procedure calls (RPC/ ALPC). Resource consumption can include kernel pool memory, CPU and handle usage. Corruption signs can include heap and pool corruption, and freeing the same memory twice. Special processes can include Windows Error Reporting (*WerFault.exe*).

Pattern Classification

http://www.dumpanalysis.org/memory-dump-analysis-pattern-classification

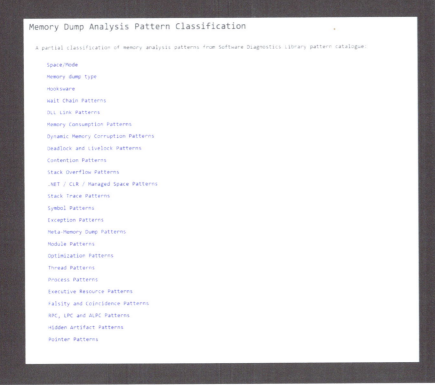

Users of Software Diagnostics Library have access to pattern catalog, advanced pattern classification, and pattern subcatalogs. Also available in Encyclopedia of Crash Dump Analysis Patterns, see Reference Resources.

http://www.dumpanalysis.org/memory-dump-analysis-pattern-classification

Example: Blocked Thread

```
THREAD ffff930ac49d0080  Cid 1ffc.109c  Teb: 0000003c7ecd1000 Win32Thread: ffff930ac62b44b0 WAIT: (WrUserRequest) UserMode Non-Alertable
        ffff930ac621fc80  QueueObject
    Not impersonating
    DeviceMap                ffffcf8978c103a0
    Owning Process           ffff930ac55de080      Image:        ApplicationA.exe
    Attached Process         N/A          Image:     N/A
    Wait Start TickCount     49071        Ticks: 976 (0:00:00:15.250)
    Context Switch Count     548          IdealProcessor: 1
    UserTime                 00:00:00.031
    KernelTime               00:00:00.015
    Win32 Start Address ApplicationA (0x00007ff64ed42c2c)
    Stack Init ffffef8637e84c90 Current ffffef8637e84490
    Base ffffef8637e85000 Limit ffffef8637e7f000 Call 0000000000000000
    Priority 10 BasePriority 8 PriorityDecrement 0 IoPriority 2 PagePriority 5
    Child-SP          RetAddr           Call Site
    ffffef86`37e844d0 fffff800`1151507d nt!KiSwapContext+0x76
    ffffef86`37e84610 fffff800`11513f04 nt!KiSwapThread+0xbfd
    ffffef86`37e846b0 fffff800`115136a5 nt!KiCommitThreadWait+0x144
    ffffef86`37e84750 fffff800`114dea6e nt!KeWaitForSingleObject+0x255
    ffffef86`37e84830 ffffdfa3`9b92962e nt!KeWaitForMultipleObjects+0x54e
    ffffef86`37e84940 ffffdfa3`9b929c55 win32kfull!xxxRealSleepThread+0x2be
    ffffef86`37e84a70 ffffdfa3`9b91c225 win32kfull!xxxSleepThread2+0xb5
    ffffef86`37e84ac0 fffff800`115d3c15 win32kfull!NtUserWaitMessage+0x65
    ffffef86`37e84b00 00007ffc`3fb71224 nt!KiSystemServiceCopyEnd+0x25 (TrapFrame @ ffffef86`37e84b00)
    0000003c`7f3ff748 00007ffc`4083bf90 win32u!NtUserWaitMessage+0x14
    0000003c`7f3ff750 00007ffc`4083bcff USER32!DialogBox2+0x260
    0000003c`7f3ff7f0 00007ffc`40882f99 USER32!InternalDialogBox+0x11b
    0000003c`7f3ff850 00007ffc`408819d5 USER32!SoftModalMessageBox+0x7e9
    0000003c`7f3ff9a0 00007ffc`40882712 USER32!MessageBoxWorker+0x319
    0000003c`7f3ffb50 00007ffc`4088279e USER32!MessageBoxTimeoutW+0x192
>>> 0000003c`7f3ffc50 00007ffc`3d2b23ff USER32!MessageBoxW+0x4e
    0000003c`7f3ffc90 00007ff6`4ed41299 apphelp!MbHook_MessageBoxW+0x2f
    0000003c`7f3ffce0 00007ff6`4ed42c89 ApplicationA+0x1299
    0000003c`7f3ffd10 00007ffc`41937bd4 ApplicationA+0x2c89
    0000003c`7f3ffd40 00007ffc`425cce51 KERNEL32!BaseThreadInitThunk+0x14
    0000003c`7f3ffd70 00000000`00000000 ntdll!RtlUserThreadStart+0x21
```

To Be Discussed Later

Complete Dump Analysis Exercise

Now I show you a few fragments from the log file you can later download after you get this presentation slides.

Example: Wait Chain

To Be Discussed Later

Complete Dump Analysis Exercise

```
THREAD ffff930ac2a850c0  Cid 1da4.0aa0  Teb: 0000005d75b4d000 Win32Thread: 0000000000000000 WAIT: (UserRequest) UserMode Non-Alertable
>>>        ffff930ac4f05ad0  Mutant - owning thread ffff930ac230f080
    Not impersonating
    DeviceMap                 ffffcf8978c103a0
    Owning Process            ffff930ac236e080         Image:          ApplicationC.exe
    Attached Process          N/A              Image:         N/A
    Wait Start TickCount      42255            Ticks: 7792 (0:00:02:01.750)
    Context Switch Count      6                IdealProcessor: 0
    UserTime                  00:00:00.000
    KernelTime                00:00:00.000
    Win32 Start Address ApplicationC (0x00007ff7b8f62ce0)
    Stack Init ffffef8637ebcc90 Current ffffef8637ebc6e0
    Base ffffef8637ebd000 Limit ffffef8637eb7000 Call 0000000000000000
    Priority 9 BasePriority 8 PriorityDecrement 0 IoPriority 2 PagePriority 5
    Child-SP          RetAddr           Call Site
    ffffef86`37ebc720 fffff800`1151507d nt!KiSwapContext+0x76
    ffffef86`37ebc860 fffff800`11513f04 nt!KiSwapThread+0xbfd
    ffffef86`37ebc900 fffff800`115136a5 nt!KiCommitThreadWait+0x144
    ffffef86`37ebc9a0 fffff800`11abd2bb nt!KeWaitForSingleObject+0x255
    ffffef86`37ebca80 fffff800`115d3c15 nt!NtWaitForSingleObject+0x10b
    ffffef86`37ebcb00 00007ffc`425fc0f4 nt!KiSystemServiceCopyEnd+0x25 (TrapFrame @ ffffef86`37ebcb00)
    0000005d`763ffdb8 00007ffc`3f8a8b03 ntdll!NtWaitForSingleObject+0x14
    0000005d`763ffdc0 00007ff7`b8f6136c KERNELBASE!WaitForSingleObjectEx+0x93
    0000005d`763ffe60 00007ff7`b8f62d3d ApplicationC+0x136c
    0000005d`763ffea0 00007ffc`41937bd4 ApplicationC+0x2d3d
    0000005d`763ffed0 00007ffc`425cce51 KERNEL32!BaseThreadInitThunk+0x14
    0000005d`763fff00 00000000`00000000 ntdll!RtlUserThreadStart+0x21
```

Example: Consumption

To Be Discussed Later

Complete Dump Analysis
Exercise

```
0: kd> !process 0 0
**** NT ACTIVE PROCESS DUMP ****
PROCESS ffff930abce80040
    SessionId: none  Cid: 0004    Peb: 00000000  ParentCid: 0000
    DirBase: 001ad002  ObjectTable: ffffcf896e606580  HandleCount: 3423.
    Image: System

PROCESS ffff930abcee2080
    SessionId: none  Cid: 0058    Peb: 00000000  ParentCid: 0004
    DirBase: 00222002  ObjectTable: ffffcf896e60ca80  HandleCount:   0.
    Image: Registry

PROCESS ffff930ac005a040
    SessionId: none  Cid: 0144    Peb: 8ed0d35000  ParentCid: 0004
    DirBase: 1006ed002  ObjectTable: ffffcf896ec2ab00  HandleCount:  53.
    Image: smss.exe

PROCESS ffff930ac015f080
    SessionId: 0  Cid: 01a0    Peb: e57797b000  ParentCid: 0198
    DirBase: 1056b0002  ObjectTable: ffffcf896ec2b7c0  HandleCount: 512.
    Image: csrss.exe

[...]

PROCESS ffff930ac2be5080
    SessionId: 1  Cid: 0c58    Peb: 56ece5a000  ParentCid: 1600
>>> DirBase: 86166002  ObjectTable: ffffcf897a694bc0  HandleCount: 20055.
    Image: ApplicationE.exe

[...]
```

Example: Corruption

To Be Discussed Later

Complete Dump Analysis
Exercise

```
THREAD ffff930ac4dda500  Cid 1df8.0714  Teb: 0000000000712000 Win32Thread: 0000000000000000 WAIT: (UserRequest) UserMode Alertable
        ffff930ac268bb60  NotificationEvent
        ffff930ac61f7080  ProcessObject
    Not impersonating
    DeviceMap               ffffcf8978c103a0
    Owning Process          ffff930ac63230c0      Image:        ApplicationD.exe
    Attached Process        N/A            Image:        N/A
    Wait Start TickCount    42613          Ticks: 7434 (0:00:01:56.156)
    Context Switch Count    16             IdealProcessor: 0
    UserTime                00:00:00.000
    KernelTime              00:00:00.000
    Win32 Start Address ApplicationD (0x00007ff625ec1318)
    Stack Init ffffef8637f6bc90 Current ffffef8637f6af30
    Base ffffef8637f6c000 Limit ffffef8637f66000 Call 0000000000000000
    Priority 9 BasePriority 8 PriorityDecrement 0 IoPriority 2 PagePriority 5
    Child-SP          RetAddr           Call Site
    ffffef86`37f6af70 fffff800`1151507d nt!KiSwapContext+0x76
    ffffef86`37f6b0b0 fffff800`11513f04 nt!KiSwapThread+0xbfd
    ffffef86`37f6b150 fffff800`114de7a7 nt!KiCommitThreadWait+0x144
    ffffef86`37f6b1f0 fffff800`11a90659 nt!KeWaitForMultipleObjects+0x287
    ffffef86`37f6b300 fffff800`11a90375 nt!ObWaitForMultipleObjects+0x2a9
    ffffef86`37f6b800 fffff800`115d3c15 nt!NtWaitForMultipleObjects+0x105
    ffffef86`37f6ba90 00007ffc`425fcbc4 nt!KiSystemServiceCopyEnd+0x25 (TrapFrame @ ffffef86`37f6bb00)
    [...]
    00000000`00f9e7a0 00007ffc`425c9fc3 ntdll!RtlDispatchException+0x219
    00000000`00f9eeb0 00007ffc`42659229 ntdll!RtlRaiseException+0x153
    00000000`00f9f6a0 00007ffc`426591f3 ntdll!RtlReportFatalFailure+0x9
    00000000`00f9f6f0 00007ffc`426615e2 ntdll!RtlReportCriticalFailure+0x97
    00000000`00f9f7e0 00007ffc`4266618ea ntdll!RtlpHeapHandleError+0x12
    00000000`00f9f810 00007ffc`4266a8a9 ntdll!RtlpHpHeapHandleError+0x7a
    00000000`00f9f840 00007ffc`425a080d ntdll!RtlpLogHeapFailure+0x45
    00000000`00f9f870 00007ffc`4259fb91 ntdll!RtlpFreeHeapInternal+0x80d
    00000000`00f9f920 00007ff6`25ec1274 ntdll!RtlFreeHeap+0x51
    00000000`00f9f960 00007ff6`25ec10c3 ApplicationD+0x1274
    [...]
```

27

Example: Special Process

```
0: kd> !vm

[...]

      564 svchost.exe                6264 Kb      1980 Kb      0 Kb
      8c8 svchost.exe                6060 Kb      2692 Kb      0 Kb
      a74 spoolsv.exe                5868 Kb      1988 Kb      0 Kb
      be4 svchost.exe                5700 Kb      2068 Kb      0 Kb
     10ac svchost.exe                5672 Kb      2232 Kb      0 Kb
>>>   bd8 WerFault.exe               5384 Kb      4944 Kb      0 Kb
     1128 svchost.exe                4968 Kb      2264 Kb      0 Kb
      274 services.exe               4916 Kb       356 Kb      0 Kb
      c28 svchost.exe                4860 Kb      2260 Kb      0 Kb
       b0 cmd.exe                    4692 Kb       356 Kb      0 Kb
     1290 browser_broker.exe         4520 Kb      2564 Kb      0 Kb
     1fbc MicrosoftEdgeSH.exe        4480 Kb      5052 Kb      0 Kb
      6dc svchost.exe                4456 Kb      1936 Kb      0 Kb
      84c svchost.exe                4292 Kb      1952 Kb      0 Kb
      e5c NisSrv.exe                 4288 Kb      2000 Kb      0 Kb
     1c44 svchost.exe                4276 Kb      1984 Kb      0 Kb
      c5c svchost.exe                4164 Kb      1980 Kb      0 Kb
     12f4 backgroundTaskHost.exe     4060 Kb      2812 Kb      0 Kb
      e94 dllhost.exe                4012 Kb      1976 Kb      0 Kb
     16b8 svchost.exe                3980 Kb      2692 Kb      0 Kb
     1ce8 ctfmon.exe                 3728 Kb      3512 Kb      0 Kb

[...]
```

To Be Discussed Later

Complete Dump Analysis Exercise

Common Mistakes

- Not switching to the appropriate context
- Not looking at full stack traces
- Not looking at all stack traces
- Not using checklists
- Not looking past the first found evidence
- Not comparing to the reference debugger output
- Not doing explicit symbol qualification: module!symbol

Note: Listing both x86 and x64 stack traces (WinDbg.org)

```
.load wow64exts
!for_each_thread "!thread @#Thread 16;.thread /w @#Thread; .reload; kv 256; .effmach AMD64"
```

The first mistake is when we forget to apply switches or flags to the WinDbg process and thread view and switch commands. The second mistake is when we forget that some commands show only partial stack traces based on the default number of stack frames to display. The third mistake is when we look only at a subset of processes. Other mistakes are evident except for the last one. Sometimes we need to explicitly qualify symbols when we have both 32-bit and 64-bit modules loaded at the same time, such as **ntdll**. Also, as we would see during exercise, most of the time, we would need to list both 32-bit and 64-bit stack traces. You can use a script that can also be found on WinDbg.org.

http://www.windbg.org/

Agenda (Exercise)

- Run processes that model abnormal behavior
- Generate a complete memory dump
- **Analyze the memory dump**

Note: I did not make a complete memory dump downloadable. You can generate your own complete memory dump after downloading and running model applications

The approach I devised for this presentation is to run a few specially constructed applications that model abnormal software behavior. The first two steps I did before the presentation, and I also pre-analyzed a memory dump by running a few commands and saving the output in a log file that I make available for download after this presentation.

Exercise: Run Processes

These processes model specific patterns:

ApplicationA, ApplicationB, ApplicationC, ApplicationD, ApplicationE
For demonstration I run x64 versions plus x86 version of ApplicationA

Note: Run applications in alphabetical order

Can be downloaded from this location:
http://www.patterndiagnostics.com/Training/Webinars/FCMDA-Examples.zip
There are x86 and x64 versions

I chose generic application names to hide what these applications are doing and also make them visible to differentiate them from OS and other 3rd-party modules.

ApplicationA: Blocked Thread and Message Box
ApplicationB and **ApplicationC:** Wait Chain
ApplicationD: Dynamic Memory Corruption (Process Heap) and Special Process
ApplicationE: Insufficient Memory (Handle Leak) and Spiking Thread

https://www.patterndiagnostics.com/Training/Webinars/FCMDA-Examples.zip

Exercise: Force A Dump

The system is x64 Windows 10

We use the following command:
C:\Tools>notmyfault64.exe /crash

Note: Wait at least 10 seconds after running model applications to have them properly initialize their dependencies

In the first version of this presentation, I used the NotMyFault Sysinternals tool. For the second version, I decided to use a more straightforward approach by killing the session 0 *csrss.exe* process. For this edition, I reverted to using the NotMyFault tool again. The previous demonstration used x64 Windows Server 2008 R2, and the second used x64 Windows 7. The third edition resued the same dump file. For this edition, I created the new dump file from x64 Windows 10.

Exercise: Dump Analysis

Now I switch to a WinDbg session...

WinDbg log from a complete memory dump:
https://www.patterndiagnostics.com/files/fpma.txt

WinDbg log (scripting both 32-bit and 64-bit stack traces):
https://www.patterndiagnostics.com/files/fpma-full.txt

0. We open a dump:

```
Microsoft (R) Windows Debugger Version 10.0.18362.1 AMD64
Copyright (c) Microsoft Corporation. All rights reserved.


Loading Dump File [C:\FPMA\MEMORY.DMP]
Kernel Bitmap Dump File: Full address space is available

Symbol search path is: srv*
Executable search path is:
Windows 10 Kernel Version 18362 MP (2 procs) Free x64
Product: WinNt, suite: TerminalServer SingleUserTS Personal
Built by: 18362.1.amd64fre.19h1_release.190318-1202
Machine Name:
Kernel base = 0xfffff800`11400000 PsLoadedModuleList = 0xfffff800`11848150
Debug session time: Thu Jun 25 21:38:59.328 2020 (UTC + 1:00)
System Uptime: 0 days 0:13:01.987
Loading Kernel Symbols
...............................................................Page 200003190 too large to be in the dump
file.
.
...............................................................
...............................................................
....
Loading User Symbols
............................
Loading unloaded module list
.......
For analysis of this file, run !analyze -v
```

1. Then we check the current process context:

```
0: kd> !process
PROCESS ffff930ac50df4c0
    SessionId: 1  Cid: 15ae4    Peb: ebacd37000  ParentCid: 00b0
    DirBase: 977e3002  ObjectTable: ffffcf898339be80  HandleCount: 123.
    Image: notmyfault64.exe
    VadRoot ffff930ac9130840 Vads 56 Clone 0 Private 307. Modified 7. Locked 0.
    DeviceMap ffffcf8979359400
    Token                             ffffcf89838a46c0
    ElapsedTime                       00:00:00.116
    UserTime                          00:00:00.000
    KernelTime                        00:00:00.000
    QuotaPoolUsage[PagedPool]         136872
    QuotaPoolUsage[NonPagedPool]      8040
    Working Set Sizes (now,min,max)  (1692, 50, 345) (6768KB, 200KB, 1380KB)
    PeakWorkingSetSize                1636
    VirtualSize                       4197 Mb
    PeakVirtualSize                   4197 Mb
    PageFaultCount                    1726
    MemoryPriority                    BACKGROUND
    BasePriority                      8
    CommitCharge                      355

        THREAD ffff930ac6077080  Cid 15ae4.1138  Teb: 000000ebacd38000 Win32Thread: ffff930ac9136f10 RUNNING on processor 0
        THREAD ffff930ac15b6080  Cid 15ae4.15bd0  Teb: 000000ebacd3a000 Win32Thread: 0000000000000000 WAIT: (WrQueue) UserMode Alertable
            ffff930ac5a6e900  QueueObject

        THREAD ffff930ac26dd080  Cid 15ae4.1a6c  Teb: 000000ebacd3c000 Win32Thread: 0000000000000000 WAIT: (WrQueue) UserMode Alertable
            ffff930ac5a6e900  QueueObject
```

2. Then we list user space modules:

```
0: kd> lmu
start             end               module name
00007ff7`89d90000 00007ff7`89dd2000  notmyfault64   (deferred)
00007ffc`34200000 00007ffc`34485000  COMCTL32       (deferred)
00007ffc`3d270000 00007ffc`3d2ff000  apphelp        (deferred)
00007ffc`3f420000 00007ffc`3f430000  UMPDC          (deferred)
00007ffc`3f430000 00007ffc`3f441000  kernel_appcore    (deferred)
00007ffc`3f450000 00007ffc`3f49a000  powrprof       (deferred)
00007ffc`3f4c0000 00007ffc`3f4e3000  profapi        (deferred)
00007ffc`3f640000 00007ffc`3f73a000  ucrtbase       (deferred)
00007ffc`3f740000 00007ffc`3f78a000  cfgmgr32       (deferred)
00007ffc`3f790000 00007ffc`3f810000  bcryptPrimitives    (deferred)
00007ffc`3f870000 00007ffc`3fb13000  KERNELBASE     (deferred)
```

```
00007ffc`3fb50000 00007ffc`3fb67000   cryptsp    (deferred)
00007ffc`3fb70000 00007ffc`3fb91000   win32u     (deferred)
00007ffc`3fba0000 00007ffc`3fd34000   gdi32full  (deferred)
00007ffc`3fd40000 00007ffc`404c0000   windows_storage   (deferred)
00007ffc`40570000 00007ffc`4060e000   msvcp_win  (deferred)
00007ffc`40810000 00007ffc`409a4000   USER32     (deferred)
00007ffc`409b0000 00007ffc`409de000   IMM32      (deferred)
00007ffc`409e0000 00007ffc`40d16000   combase    (deferred)
00007ffc`40f50000 00007ffc`41070000   RPCRT4     (deferred)
00007ffc`41070000 00007ffc`410c2000   SHLWAPI    (deferred)
00007ffc`410d0000 00007ffc`41167000   sechost    (deferred)
00007ffc`411d0000 00007ffc`41273000   advapi32   (deferred)
00007ffc`413d0000 00007ffc`414a0000   COMDLG32   (deferred)
00007ffc`41920000 00007ffc`419d2000   KERNEL32   (deferred)
00007ffc`41a50000 00007ffc`42135000   SHELL32    (deferred)
00007ffc`423a0000 00007ffc`4243e000   msvcrt     (deferred)
00007ffc`42440000 00007ffc`42466000   GDI32      (deferred)
00007ffc`42470000 00007ffc`42519000   shcore     (deferred)
00007ffc`42560000 00007ffc`42750000   ntdll      (pdb symbols)        C:\ProgramData\dbg\sym\ntdll.pdb\
FB9DAFFD71C49D3C81344D29E038B4251\ntdll.pdb
```

3. And list kernel space modules:

```
0: kd> lmk
start             end                 module name
ffffdfa3`9b800000 ffffdfa3`9bba2000   win32kfull   (deferred)
ffffdfa3`9bd10000 ffffdfa3`9bd9c000   win32k       (deferred)
ffffdfa3`9bff0000 ffffdfa3`9c296000   win32kbase   (deferred)
ffffdfa3`9c2a0000 ffffdfa3`9c2e8000   cdd          (deferred)
fffff800`1135c000 fffff800`11400000   hal          (deferred)
fffff800`11400000 fffff800`11eb7000   nt           (pdb symbols)        C:\ProgramData\dbg\sym\ntkrnlmp.pdb\
BE3E0FF92C7A93433D4A950A037EF6561\ntkrnlmp.pdb
fffff800`13800000 fffff800`1380b000   kd           (deferred)
fffff800`13810000 fffff800`13a11000   mcupdate_GenuineIntel   (deferred)
fffff800`13a20000 fffff800`13a31000   werkernel    (deferred)
fffff800`13a40000 fffff800`13a6a000   ksecdd       (deferred)
fffff800`13a70000 fffff800`13ad0000   msrpc        (deferred)
fffff800`13ae0000 fffff800`13b07000   tm           (deferred)
fffff800`13b10000 fffff800`13b78000   CLFS         (deferred)
fffff800`13b80000 fffff800`13b9a000   PSHED        (deferred)
fffff800`13ba0000 fffff800`13bab000   BOOTVID      (deferred)
fffff800`13bb0000 fffff800`13cb5000   clipsp       (deferred)
fffff800`13cc0000 fffff800`13d31000   FLTMGR       (deferred)
fffff800`13d40000 fffff800`13d4e000   cmimcext     (deferred)
fffff800`13d50000 fffff800`13d5c000   ntosext      (deferred)
fffff800`13d60000 fffff800`13e3d000   CI           (deferred)
fffff800`13e40000 fffff800`13efc000   cng          (deferred)
fffff800`13f00000 fffff800`13fd5000   Wdf01000     (deferred)
fffff800`13fe0000 fffff800`13ff3000   WDFLDR       (deferred)
fffff800`14000000 fffff800`1400f000   SleepStudyHelper   (deferred)
fffff800`14010000 fffff800`14020000   WppRecorder  (deferred)
fffff800`14030000 fffff800`14055000   acpiex       (deferred)
fffff800`14060000 fffff800`1407a000   SgrmAgent    (deferred)
fffff800`14080000 fffff800`1414c000   ACPI         (deferred)
fffff800`14150000 fffff800`1415c000   WMILIB       (deferred)
fffff800`14180000 fffff800`141db000   intelpep     (deferred)
fffff800`141e0000 fffff800`141f7000   WindowsTrustedRT   (deferred)
fffff800`14200000 fffff800`1420b000   WindowsTrustedRTProxy   (deferred)
fffff800`14210000 fffff800`14225000   pcw          (deferred)
fffff800`14230000 fffff800`1423b000   msisadrv     (deferred)
fffff800`14240000 fffff800`142af000   pci          (deferred)
fffff800`142b0000 fffff800`142c3000   vdrvroot     (deferred)
fffff800`142d0000 fffff800`14311000   ucx01000     (deferred)
fffff800`14320000 fffff800`14353000   pdc          (deferred)
fffff800`14360000 fffff800`14379000   CEA          (deferred)
fffff800`14380000 fffff800`143b0000   partmgr      (deferred)
fffff800`143c0000 fffff800`14465000   spaceport    (deferred)
fffff800`14470000 fffff800`1447b000   intelide     (deferred)
fffff800`14480000 fffff800`14493000   PCIIDEX      (deferred)
fffff800`144a0000 fffff800`144ba000   volmgr       (deferred)
fffff800`144c0000 fffff800`1450e000   sdbus        (deferred)
fffff800`14510000 fffff800`14573000   volmgrx      (deferred)
fffff800`14580000 fffff800`14598000   vsock        (deferred)
```

35

```
fffff800`145a0000 fffff800`145bc000   vmci        (deferred)
fffff800`145c0000 fffff800`145d8000   urscx01000    (deferred)
fffff800`145e0000 fffff800`145ff000   mountmgr    (deferred)
fffff800`14600000 fffff800`1461f000   lsi_sas     (deferred)
fffff800`14620000 fffff800`146c2000   storport    (deferred)
fffff800`146d0000 fffff800`146dd000   atapi       (deferred)
fffff800`146e0000 fffff800`1471b000   ataport     (deferred)
fffff800`14720000 fffff800`1474e000   storahci    (deferred)
fffff800`14750000 fffff800`1476b000   EhStorClass    (deferred)
fffff800`14770000 fffff800`1478a000   fileinfo    (deferred)
fffff800`14790000 fffff800`147cd000   Wof         (deferred)
fffff800`147d0000 fffff800`147de000   USBD        (deferred)
fffff800`147e0000 fffff800`147ed000   urschipidea    (deferred)
fffff800`147f0000 fffff800`147fd000   Fs_Rec      (deferred)
fffff800`14800000 fffff800`14865000   WdFilter    (deferred)
fffff800`14870000 fffff800`14b0d000   Ntfs        (deferred)
fffff800`14b10000 fffff800`14b43000   usbccgp     (deferred)
fffff800`14b50000 fffff800`14b6d000   usbehci     (deferred)
fffff800`14b70000 fffff800`14bea000   USBPORT     (deferred)
fffff800`14bf0000 fffff800`14c7a000   usbhub      (deferred)
fffff800`14c80000 fffff800`14d1c000   UsbHub3     (deferred)
fffff800`14d20000 fffff800`14e92000   ndis        (deferred)
fffff800`14ea0000 fffff800`14f34000   NETIO       (deferred)
fffff800`14f40000 fffff800`14f72000   ksecpkg     (deferred)
fffff800`14f80000 fffff800`15269000   tcpip       (deferred)
fffff800`15270000 fffff800`152ea000   fwpkclnt    (deferred)
fffff800`152f0000 fffff800`15320000   wfplwfs     (deferred)
fffff800`15330000 fffff800`153f9000   fvevol      (deferred)
fffff800`15400000 fffff800`1540b000   volume      (deferred)
fffff800`15410000 fffff800`1547d000   volsnap     (deferred)
fffff800`15480000 fffff800`15509000   USBXHCI     (deferred)
fffff800`15510000 fffff800`15535000   USBSTOR     (deferred)
fffff800`15540000 fffff800`15558000   uaspstor    (deferred)
fffff800`15560000 fffff800`1557e000   sdstor      (deferred)
fffff800`15580000 fffff800`155ce000   rdyboost    (deferred)
fffff800`155d0000 fffff800`155f5000   mup         (deferred)
fffff800`15600000 fffff800`15612000   iorate      (deferred)
fffff800`15640000 fffff800`1565c000   disk        (deferred)
fffff800`15660000 fffff800`156cb000   CLASSPNP    (deferred)
fffff800`15c00000 fffff800`15c3b000   HIDCLASS    (deferred)
fffff800`15c40000 fffff800`15c53000   HIDPARSE    (deferred)
fffff800`15c60000 fffff800`15c75000   filecrypt    (deferred)
fffff800`15c80000 fffff800`15c8e000   tbs         (deferred)
fffff800`15c90000 fffff800`15c9a000   Null        (deferred)
fffff800`15ca0000 fffff800`15caa000   Beep        (deferred)
fffff800`15cb0000 fffff800`15cc0000   vmrawdsk    (deferred)
fffff800`15cd0000 fffff800`16043000   dxgkrnl     (deferred)
fffff800`16050000 fffff800`16066000   watchdog    (deferred)
fffff800`16070000 fffff800`16086000   BasicDisplay    (deferred)
fffff800`16090000 fffff800`1611c000   Vid         (deferred)
fffff800`16120000 fffff800`1613f000   winhvr      (deferred)
fffff800`16140000 fffff800`16151000   CompositeBus    (deferred)
fffff800`16160000 fffff800`1616d000   kdnic       (deferred)
fffff800`16170000 fffff800`16185000   umbus       (deferred)
fffff800`16190000 fffff800`161b3000   i8042prt    (deferred)
fffff800`161c0000 fffff800`161d4000   kbdclass    (deferred)
fffff800`161e0000 fffff800`161e9000   vmmouse     (deferred)
fffff800`161f0000 fffff800`16203000   mouclass    (deferred)
fffff800`16210000 fffff800`1622c000   serial      (deferred)
fffff800`16230000 fffff800`1623f000   serenum     (deferred)
fffff800`16240000 fffff800`1624a000   vm3dmp_loader    (deferred)
fffff800`16250000 fffff800`1629b000   vm3dmp      (deferred)
fffff800`162a0000 fffff800`162b1000   usbuhci     (deferred)
fffff800`162c0000 fffff800`162e2000   HDAudBus    (deferred)
fffff800`162f0000 fffff800`16357000   portcls     (deferred)
fffff800`16360000 fffff800`16381000   drmk        (deferred)
fffff800`16390000 fffff800`16408000   ks          (deferred)
fffff800`16410000 fffff800`1649e000   e1i65x64    (deferred)
fffff800`164a0000 fffff800`164ab000   vmgencounter    (deferred)
fffff800`164b0000 fffff800`164bf000   CmBatt      (deferred)
fffff800`164c0000 fffff800`164d0000   BATTC       (deferred)
fffff800`164e0000 fffff800`1651e000   intelppm    (deferred)
fffff800`16520000 fffff800`16531000   BasicRender    (deferred)
fffff800`16540000 fffff800`1654d000   NdisVirtualBus    (deferred)
fffff800`16550000 fffff800`16560000   mssmbios    (deferred)
fffff800`16570000 fffff800`1657c000   swenum      (deferred)
fffff800`16580000 fffff800`1658e000   rdpbus      (deferred)
fffff800`16590000 fffff800`165fe000   HdAudio     (deferred)
```

```
fffff800`16600000 fffff800`1660f000    ksthunk     (deferred)
fffff800`16610000 fffff800`16620000    mouhid      (deferred)
fffff800`16630000 fffff800`16639000    vmusbmouse    (deferred)
fffff800`16640000 fffff800`16651000    Msfs        (deferred)
fffff800`16660000 fffff800`16686000    tdx         (deferred)
fffff800`166c0000 fffff800`166dd000    crashdmp    (deferred)
fffff800`166e0000 fffff800`16718000    winquic     (deferred)
fffff800`16780000 fffff800`167b0000    cdrom       (deferred)
fffff800`167c0000 fffff800`167d2000    hidusb      (deferred)
fffff800`167e0000 fffff800`167fc000    Npfs        (deferred)
fffff800`16800000 fffff800`16813000    afunix      (deferred)
fffff800`16820000 fffff800`168c7000    afd         (deferred)
fffff800`168d0000 fffff800`168ea000    vwififlt    (deferred)
fffff800`168f0000 fffff800`1691b000    pacer       (deferred)
fffff800`16920000 fffff800`16934000    netbios     (deferred)
fffff800`16940000 fffff800`169bb000    rdbss       (deferred)
fffff800`169c0000 fffff800`169d2000    nsiproxy    (deferred)
fffff800`169e0000 fffff800`169ed000    npsvctrig    (deferred)
fffff800`169f0000 fffff800`169fa000    gpuenergydrv    (deferred)
fffff800`16a00000 fffff800`16a2c000    dfsc        (deferred)
fffff800`16a50000 fffff800`16abb000    fastfat     (deferred)
fffff800`16ac0000 fffff800`16ad6000    bam         (deferred)
fffff800`16ae0000 fffff800`16b2f000    ahcache     (deferred)
fffff800`16b30000 fffff800`16b4f000    BTHUSB      (deferred)
fffff800`16b50000 fffff800`16cb4000    bthport     (deferred)
fffff800`16cc0000 fffff800`16cfa000    rfcomm      (deferred)
fffff800`16d00000 fffff800`16d22000    BthEnum     (deferred)
fffff800`16d30000 fffff800`16d56000    bthpan      (deferred)
fffff800`16d70000 fffff800`16d7e000    dump_diskdump    (deferred)
fffff800`16da0000 fffff800`16dbf000    dump_lsi_sas    (deferred)
fffff800`16de0000 fffff800`16dfd000    dump_dumpfve    (deferred)
fffff800`16e00000 fffff800`16eda000    dxgmms2     (deferred)
fffff800`16ee0000 fffff800`16f30000    WUDFRd      (deferred)
fffff800`16f40000 fffff800`16f6a000    luafv       (deferred)
fffff800`16f70000 fffff800`16fa7000    wcifs       (deferred)
fffff800`16fb0000 fffff800`17027000    cldflt      (deferred)
fffff800`17030000 fffff800`1704a000    storqosflt    (deferred)
fffff800`17050000 fffff800`17068000    lltdio      (deferred)
fffff800`17070000 fffff800`17089000    mslldp      (deferred)
fffff800`17090000 fffff800`170ab000    rspndr      (deferred)
fffff800`170b0000 fffff800`17121000    dxgmms1     (deferred)
fffff800`17130000 fffff800`17148000    monitor     (deferred)
fffff800`17150000 fffff800`1716d000    wanarp      (deferred)
fffff800`17170000 fffff800`17180000    TDI         (deferred)
fffff800`17190000 fffff800`1719e000    ws2ifsl     (deferred)
fffff800`171a0000 fffff800`171f9000    netbt       (deferred)
fffff800`17400000 fffff800`17414000    mmcss       (deferred)
fffff800`17420000 fffff800`174e5000    srv2        (deferred)
fffff800`174f0000 fffff800`17542000    mrxsmb10    (deferred)
fffff800`17550000 fffff800`17577000    Ndu         (deferred)
fffff800`17580000 fffff800`17656000    peauth      (deferred)
fffff800`17660000 fffff800`17674000    tcpipreg    (deferred)
fffff800`17680000 fffff800`1769d000    rassstp     (deferred)
fffff800`176a0000 fffff800`176e1000    NDProxy     (deferred)
fffff800`176f0000 fffff800`1771b000    vmhgfs      (deferred)
fffff800`17720000 fffff800`17747000    AgileVpn    (deferred)
fffff800`17750000 fffff800`17772000    rasl2tp     (deferred)
fffff800`17780000 fffff800`177a0000    raspptp     (deferred)
fffff800`177b0000 fffff800`177cc000    raspppoe    (deferred)
fffff800`177d0000 fffff800`177df000    ndistapi    (deferred)
fffff800`177e0000 fffff800`1781a000    ndiswan     (deferred)
fffff800`17820000 fffff800`17835000    WdNisDrv    (deferred)
fffff800`17840000 fffff800`17853000    condrv      (deferred)
fffff800`17860000 fffff800`17868000    myfault     (deferred)
fffff800`17f10000 fffff800`18054000    HTTP        (deferred)
fffff800`18060000 fffff800`18085000    bowser      (deferred)
fffff800`18090000 fffff800`180aa000    mpsdrv      (deferred)
fffff800`180b0000 fffff800`1813f000    mrxsmb      (deferred)
fffff800`18140000 fffff800`18185000    mrxsmb20    (deferred)
fffff800`18190000 fffff800`1819a000    vmmemctl    (deferred)
fffff800`181a0000 fffff800`181f3000    srvnet      (deferred)

Unloaded modules:
fffff800`166f0000 fffff800`166ff000    dump_storport.sys
fffff800`16720000 fffff800`16740000    dump_lsi_sas.sys
fffff800`16760000 fffff800`1677e000    dump_dumpfve.sys
fffff800`16a30000 fffff800`16a4e000    dam.sys
fffff800`16640000 fffff800`16691000    WUDFRd.sys
```

37

```
fffff800`14160000 fffff800`14171000   WdBoot.sys
fffff800`15620000 fffff800`15631000   hwpolicy.sys
```

4. Then we list processes:

```
0: kd> !process 0 0
**** NT ACTIVE PROCESS DUMP ****
PROCESS ffff930abce80040
    SessionId: none  Cid: 0004    Peb: 00000000  ParentCid: 0000
    DirBase: 001ad002  ObjectTable: ffffcf896e606580  HandleCount: 3423.
    Image: System

PROCESS ffff930abcee2080
    SessionId: none  Cid: 0058    Peb: 00000000  ParentCid: 0004
    DirBase: 00222002  ObjectTable: ffffcf896e60ca80  HandleCount:   0.
    Image: Registry

PROCESS ffff930ac005a040
    SessionId: none  Cid: 0144    Peb: 8ed0d35000  ParentCid: 0004
    DirBase: 1006ed002  ObjectTable: ffffcf896ec2ab00  HandleCount: 53.
    Image: smss.exe

PROCESS ffff930ac015f080
    SessionId: 0  Cid: 01a0    Peb: e57797b000  ParentCid: 0198
    DirBase: 1056b0002  ObjectTable: ffffcf896ec2b7c0  HandleCount: 512.
    Image: csrss.exe

PROCESS ffff930ac015e080
    SessionId: 0  Cid: 01e8    Peb: 6493111000  ParentCid: 0198
    DirBase: 1065fe002  ObjectTable: ffffcf89720eab00  HandleCount: 168.
    Image: wininit.exe

PROCESS ffff930ac014f080
    SessionId: 1  Cid: 01f0    Peb: b080cba000  ParentCid: 01e0
    DirBase: 1044b1002  ObjectTable: ffffcf89720eae40  HandleCount: 413.
    Image: csrss.exe

PROCESS ffff930ac0b73080
    SessionId: 1  Cid: 0244    Peb: 648f55c000  ParentCid: 01e0
    DirBase: 109e33002  ObjectTable: ffffcf89720e9d40  HandleCount: 286.
    Image: winlogon.exe

PROCESS ffff930ac0b72080
    SessionId: 0  Cid: 0274    Peb: d01717a000  ParentCid: 01e8
    DirBase: 106427002  ObjectTable: ffffcf89720ed040  HandleCount: 691.
    Image: services.exe

PROCESS ffff930ac0b84080
    SessionId: 0  Cid: 0284    Peb: 144df43000  ParentCid: 01e8
    DirBase: 10a491002  ObjectTable: ffffcf89720eb5c0  HandleCount: 1333.
    Image: lsass.exe

PROCESS ffff930ac1221240
    SessionId: 0  Cid: 02e4    Peb: d2d7a21000  ParentCid: 0274
    DirBase: 109659002  ObjectTable: ffffcf89720ec480  HandleCount: 86.
    Image: svchost.exe

PROCESS ffff930ac1232140
    SessionId: 0  Cid: 02f4    Peb: 3234e95000  ParentCid: 01e8
    DirBase: 10bb20002  ObjectTable: ffffcf89720ec6c0  HandleCount: 32.
    Image: fontdrvhost.exe

PROCESS ffff930ac12300c0
    SessionId: 1  Cid: 02fc    Peb: e89a431000  ParentCid: 0244
    DirBase: 10bbed002  ObjectTable: ffffcf89720eb900  HandleCount: 32.
    Image: fontdrvhost.exe

PROCESS ffff930ac1243240
    SessionId: 0  Cid: 0344    Peb: 4c16052000  ParentCid: 0274
    DirBase: 10bc82002  ObjectTable: ffffcf89720ee140  HandleCount: 1219.
    Image: svchost.exe

PROCESS ffff930ac124a480
    SessionId: 0  Cid: 0358    Peb: 6ef879d000  ParentCid: 0274
    DirBase: 10bff1002  ObjectTable: ffffcf89720ece40  HandleCount: 415.
    Image: WUDFHost.exe
```

```
PROCESS ffff930ac132d2c0
    SessionId: 0  Cid: 03b4    Peb: df2d879000  ParentCid: 0274
    DirBase: 10ab3b002  ObjectTable: ffffcf89723c9d40  HandleCount: 1309.
    Image: svchost.exe

PROCESS ffff930ac1379240
    SessionId: 0  Cid: 03e8    Peb: 7fa7ab1000  ParentCid: 0274
    DirBase: 10cfed002  ObjectTable: ffffcf89723ca6c0  HandleCount: 259.
    Image: svchost.exe

PROCESS ffff930ac1404080
    SessionId: 1  Cid: 01b4    Peb: 7a7039d000  ParentCid: 0244
    DirBase: 10de6f002  ObjectTable: ffffcf89723cd380  HandleCount: 913.
    Image: dwm.exe

PROCESS ffff930ac143d240
    SessionId: 0  Cid: 0318    Peb: fbaa28f000  ParentCid: 0274
    DirBase: 10e85b002  ObjectTable: ffffcf89723cc8c0  HandleCount: 189.
    Image: svchost.exe

PROCESS ffff930ac144b300
    SessionId: 0  Cid: 040c    Peb: 719c13000  ParentCid: 0274
    DirBase: 10ed1d002  ObjectTable: ffffcf89723ce580  HandleCount: 117.
    Image: svchost.exe

PROCESS ffff930ac1449380
    SessionId: 0  Cid: 0424    Peb: 64ce458000  ParentCid: 0274
    DirBase: 10cd2f002  ObjectTable: ffffcf89723cb7c0  HandleCount: 184.
    Image: svchost.exe

PROCESS ffff930ac146d2c0
    SessionId: 0  Cid: 0440    Peb: 2e116a000  ParentCid: 0274
    DirBase: 10f01f002  ObjectTable: ffffcf89723cde00  HandleCount: 167.
    Image: svchost.exe

PROCESS ffff930ac146e080
    SessionId: 0  Cid: 0448    Peb: e460187000  ParentCid: 0274
    DirBase: 10cce5002  ObjectTable: ffffcf89723ce240  HandleCount: 258.
    Image: svchost.exe

PROCESS ffff930ac146f080
    SessionId: 0  Cid: 0458    Peb: e7f946000  ParentCid: 0274
    DirBase: 10edc8002  ObjectTable: ffffcf89723cd580  HandleCount: 165.
    Image: svchost.exe

PROCESS ffff930ac1493280
    SessionId: 0  Cid: 0490    Peb: ef5b71a000  ParentCid: 0274
    DirBase: 10f34a002  ObjectTable: ffffcf89723d09c0  HandleCount: 232.
    Image: svchost.exe

PROCESS ffff930ac1496300
    SessionId: 0  Cid: 04a0    Peb: e768ce4000  ParentCid: 0274
    DirBase: 108a4b002  ObjectTable: ffffcf89723d0240  HandleCount: 170.
    Image: svchost.exe

PROCESS ffff930ac153b240
    SessionId: 0  Cid: 0564    Peb: 5b137bf000  ParentCid: 0274
    DirBase: 11074f002  ObjectTable: ffffcf89723d0880  HandleCount: 413.
    Image: svchost.exe

PROCESS ffff930ac1543300
    SessionId: 0  Cid: 0590    Peb: 5c8beaf000  ParentCid: 0274
    DirBase: 110c51002  ObjectTable: ffffcf89726746c0  HandleCount: 130.
    Image: svchost.exe

PROCESS ffff930ac157d240
    SessionId: 0  Cid: 05a4    Peb: 7eae8b6000  ParentCid: 0274
    DirBase: 110e8b002  ObjectTable: ffffcf8972674b00  HandleCount: 239.
    Image: svchost.exe

PROCESS ffff930ac15822c0
    SessionId: 0  Cid: 05b0    Peb: e0746b000  ParentCid: 0274
    DirBase: 10efef002  ObjectTable: ffffcf8972673080  HandleCount: 248.
    Image: svchost.exe

PROCESS ffff930ac153e080
    SessionId: 0  Cid: 05e8    Peb: 8b44006000  ParentCid: 0274
```

```
   DirBase: 1117e0002  ObjectTable: ffffcf89726756c0  HandleCount: 285.
   Image: svchost.exe

PROCESS ffff930ac143f080
    SessionId: 0  Cid: 05f0    Peb: 69e0abe000  ParentCid: 0274
    DirBase: 111860002  ObjectTable: ffffcf89726745c0  HandleCount: 215.
    Image: svchost.exe

PROCESS ffff930ac15b3300
    SessionId: 0  Cid: 061c    Peb: 939a414000  ParentCid: 0274
    DirBase: 110226002  ObjectTable: ffffcf8972675a00  HandleCount: 197.
    Image: svchost.exe

PROCESS ffff930ac15b5300
    SessionId: 0  Cid: 0634    Peb: 240ca79000  ParentCid: 0274
    DirBase: 112128002  ObjectTable: ffffcf8972676d00  HandleCount: 407.
    Image: svchost.exe

PROCESS ffff930ac1650480
    SessionId: 0  Cid: 0688    Peb: 7dbcc45000  ParentCid: 0274
    DirBase: 110928002  ObjectTable: ffffcf8972678240  HandleCount: 184.
    Image: svchost.exe

PROCESS ffff930ac1694240
    SessionId: 0  Cid: 06a8    Peb: 28ac893000  ParentCid: 0274
    DirBase: 110832002  ObjectTable: ffffcf89726788c0  HandleCount: 277.
    Image: svchost.exe

PROCESS ffff930ac16b22c0
    SessionId: 0  Cid: 06dc    Peb: 41dadd5000  ParentCid: 0274
    DirBase: 11399e002  ObjectTable: ffffcf8972678480  HandleCount: 139.
    Image: svchost.exe

PROCESS ffff930ac16e5300
    SessionId: 0  Cid: 0770    Peb: 52a229e000  ParentCid: 0274
    DirBase: 1144e7002  ObjectTable: ffffcf89728143c0  HandleCount: 225.
    Image: svchost.exe

PROCESS ffff930ac16df080
    SessionId: 0  Cid: 07b8    Peb: 19a7769000  ParentCid: 0274
    DirBase: 11495e002  ObjectTable: ffffcf89728132c0  HandleCount: 458.
    Image: svchost.exe

PROCESS ffff930abce7f080
    SessionId: 0  Cid: 07cc    Peb: 3dc625f000  ParentCid: 0274
    DirBase: 114bb2002  ObjectTable: ffffcf8972814c40  HandleCount: 241.
    Image: svchost.exe

PROCESS ffff930abcfb9080
    SessionId: 0  Cid: 07dc    Peb: e1780ae000  ParentCid: 0274
    DirBase: 114e8c002  ObjectTable: ffffcf89728157c0  HandleCount: 205.
    Image: svchost.exe

PROCESS ffff930abcf64040
    SessionId: none  Cid: 081c    Peb: 00000000  ParentCid: 0004
    DirBase: 1085cb002  ObjectTable: ffffcf8972818140  HandleCount:   0.
    Image: MemCompression

PROCESS ffff930abcf60080
    SessionId: 0  Cid: 084c    Peb: 889ff02000  ParentCid: 0274
    DirBase: 107f24002  ObjectTable: ffffcf8972819240  HandleCount: 385.
    Image: svchost.exe

PROCESS ffff930ac17b4300
    SessionId: 0  Cid: 0860    Peb: 4bc784d000  ParentCid: 0274
    DirBase: 107cf5002  ObjectTable: ffffcf89728177c0  HandleCount: 270.
    Image: svchost.exe

PROCESS ffff930ac17b7080
    SessionId: 0  Cid: 0870    Peb: 5bd4396000  ParentCid: 0274
    DirBase: 105e53002  ObjectTable: ffffcf897281a680  HandleCount: 186.
    Image: svchost.exe

PROCESS ffff930abcf62080
    SessionId: 0  Cid: 08a4    Peb: 38b93ea000  ParentCid: 0274
    DirBase: 106e0f002  ObjectTable: ffffcf8972819780  HandleCount: 177.
    Image: svchost.exe
```

```
PROCESS ffff930ac180a2c0
    SessionId: 0  Cid: 08c0    Peb: 11624a3000  ParentCid: 0274
    DirBase: 106dfd002  ObjectTable: ffffcf89729f53c0  HandleCount: 155.
    Image: svchost.exe

PROCESS ffff930ac18c72c0
    SessionId: 0  Cid: 0940    Peb: a1df6e6000  ParentCid: 0274
    DirBase: 118e60002  ObjectTable: ffffcf89729f5e40  HandleCount: 395.
    Image: svchost.exe

PROCESS ffff930ac1920300
    SessionId: 0  Cid: 0970    Peb: 7ec602d000  ParentCid: 0274
    DirBase: 11ac57002  ObjectTable: ffffcf89729f9140  HandleCount: 353.
    Image: svchost.exe

PROCESS ffff930ac1940300
    SessionId: 0  Cid: 09a4    Peb: 6794fa8000  ParentCid: 0274
    DirBase: 11b56c002  ObjectTable: ffffcf89729f75c0  HandleCount: 128.
    Image: svchost.exe

PROCESS ffff930ac1941080
    SessionId: 0  Cid: 09ac    Peb: f0ba940000  ParentCid: 0274
    DirBase: 11b59b002  ObjectTable: ffffcf89729f8480  HandleCount: 362.
    Image: svchost.exe

PROCESS ffff930ac1922340
    SessionId: 0  Cid: 09e8    Peb: 4f65911000  ParentCid: 0274
    DirBase: 119a36002  ObjectTable: ffffcf89729fa580  HandleCount: 273.
    Image: svchost.exe

PROCESS ffff930ac1a52240
    SessionId: 0  Cid: 0a74    Peb: 00b71000  ParcntCid: 0274
    DirBase: 11a6ec002  ObjectTable: ffffcf89729fb580  HandleCount: 457.
    Image: spoolsv.exe

PROCESS ffff930ac1a54300
    SessionId: 0  Cid: 0a8c    Peb: fb1543b000  ParentCid: 0274
    DirBase: 11deae002  ObjectTable: ffffcf89729fb480  HandleCount: 186.
    Image: svchost.exe

PROCESS ffff930ac1a92280
    SessionId: 0  Cid: 0aa4    Peb: 6fe6a05000  ParentCid: 0274
    DirBase: 11ae6b002  ObjectTable: ffffcf89729fc680  HandleCount: 217.
    Image: svchost.exe

PROCESS ffff930ac1ab2300
    SessionId: 0  Cid: 0af4    Peb: 5d3393b000  ParentCid: 0274
    DirBase: 11cbdf002  ObjectTable: ffffcf89729fc340  HandleCount: 417.
    Image: svchost.exe

PROCESS ffff930ac1a96080
    SessionId: 0  Cid: 0b18    Peb: 257d173000  ParentCid: 0274
    DirBase: 0153e002  ObjectTable: ffffcf8973013400  HandleCount: 189.
    Image: svchost.exe

PROCESS ffff930ac1bd7300
    SessionId: 0  Cid: 0be4    Peb: 1f2731b000  ParentCid: 0274
    DirBase: 13b04e002  ObjectTable: ffffcf8973015900  HandleCount: 235.
    Image: svchost.exe

PROCESS ffff930ac1bd8080
    SessionId: 0  Cid: 0bec    Peb: d6127b3000  ParentCid: 0274
    DirBase: 11f7e1002  ObjectTable: ffffcf8973016900  HandleCount: 607.
    Image: svchost.exe

PROCESS ffff930ac1bd9080
    SessionId: 0  Cid: 0bf8    Peb: ce7c1f0000  ParentCid: 0274
    DirBase: 4abcc002  ObjectTable: ffffcf89730163c0  HandleCount: 343.
    Image: svchost.exe

PROCESS ffff930ac1bda080
    SessionId: 0  Cid: 0664    Peb: 4d42121000  ParentCid: 0274
    DirBase: 11f724002  ObjectTable: ffffcf8973016d40  HandleCount: 353.
    Image: svchost.exe

PROCESS ffff930ac1c2a340
    SessionId: 0  Cid: 095c    Peb: c8e86ca000  ParentCid: 0274
    DirBase: 11fdce002  ObjectTable: ffffcf8973019280  HandleCount: 212.
```

```
      Image: svchost.exe

  PROCESS ffff930ac1c602c0
      SessionId: 0  Cid: 099c    Peb: 63642f7000  ParentCid: 0274
      DirBase: 11f6bc002  ObjectTable: ffffcf8973018180  HandleCount: 134.
      Image: svchost.exe

  PROCESS ffff930ac1c65380
      SessionId: 0  Cid: 0b40    Peb: 42de135000  ParentCid: 0274
      DirBase: 11dc5a002  ObjectTable: ffffcf89730187c0  HandleCount: 130.
      Image: svchost.exe

  PROCESS ffff930ac1c5f300
      SessionId: 0  Cid: 0c0c    Peb: 2a9b948000  ParentCid: 0274
      DirBase: 11fc81002  ObjectTable: ffffcf8973019480  HandleCount: 174.
      Image: VGAuthService.exe

  PROCESS ffff930ac1caa340
      SessionId: 0  Cid: 0c14    Peb: ade074a000  ParentCid: 0274
      DirBase: 12040f002  ObjectTable: ffffcf8973017900  HandleCount: 775.
      Image: MsMpEng.exe

  PROCESS ffff930ac1b30080
      SessionId: 0  Cid: 0c28    Peb: ebfcb9c000  ParentCid: 0274
      DirBase: 12044a002  ObjectTable: ffffcf897301b7c0  HandleCount: 417.
      Image: svchost.exe

  PROCESS ffff930ac1ca80c0
      SessionId: 0  Cid: 0c34    Peb: f7aaa23000  ParentCid: 0274
      DirBase: 12000d002  ObjectTable: ffffcf8973019c00  HandleCount: 386.
      Image: vmtoolsd.exe

  PROCESS ffff930ac1ce5240
      SessionId: 0  Cid: 0c5c    Peb: 5a4a675000  ParentCid: 0274
      DirBase: 120e62002  ObjectTable: ffffcf897301a7c0  HandleCount: 522.
      Image: svchost.exe

  PROCESS ffff930ac1d6e300
      SessionId: 0  Cid: 0cb8    Peb: 951e6b0000  ParentCid: 0274
      DirBase: 123db6002  ObjectTable: ffffcf897301c040  HandleCount: 138.
      Image: svchost.exe

  PROCESS ffff930ac1e96240
      SessionId: 0  Cid: 0da0    Peb: 6c966ab000  ParentCid: 0274
      DirBase: 124bbf002  ObjectTable: ffffcf89729fbf00  HandleCount: 378.
      Image: svchost.exe

  PROCESS ffff930ac1fe6280
      SessionId: 0  Cid: 0e94    Peb: 1bb6618000  ParentCid: 0274
      DirBase: 1266cf002  ObjectTable: ffffcf8973613e80  HandleCount: 267.
      Image: dllhost.exe

  PROCESS ffff930ac204c080
      SessionId: 0  Cid: 0f5c    Peb: af910f1000  ParentCid: 0344
      DirBase: 12bd6a002  ObjectTable: ffffcf89736175c0  HandleCount: 266.
      Image: WmiPrvSE.exe

  PROCESS ffff930ac21bf080
      SessionId: 0  Cid: 049c    Peb: 5990f83000  ParentCid: 0274
      DirBase: 12eb98002  ObjectTable: ffffcf897361a580  HandleCount: 624.
      Image: svchost.exe

  PROCESS ffff930abd1153c0
      SessionId: 0  Cid: 0e5c    Peb: c870005000  ParentCid: 0274
      DirBase: 12d993002  ObjectTable: ffffcf89736198c0  HandleCount: 195.
      Image: NisSrv.exe

  PROCESS ffff930abd130280
      SessionId: 0  Cid: 0c50    Peb: d4b3e89000  ParentCid: 0274
      DirBase: 133491002  ObjectTable: ffffcf897361c040  HandleCount: 225.
      Image: msdtc.exe

  PROCESS ffff930ac1f84080
      SessionId: 0  Cid: 1158    Peb: d3d5dc4000  ParentCid: 0274
      DirBase: 133dc5002  ObjectTable: ffffcf897361e980  HandleCount: 1034.
      Image: svchost.exe

  PROCESS ffff930abd131080
```

```
    SessionId: 0  Cid: 1230    Peb: 51044f5000  ParentCid: 0344
    DirBase: 1368f4002  ObjectTable: ffffcf897361e440  HandleCount: 310.
    Image: WmiPrvSE.exe

PROCESS ffff930ac235f080
    SessionId: 0  Cid: 125c    Peb: a7ee07000  ParentCid: 0274
    DirBase: 13a3d0002  ObjectTable: 00000000  HandleCount:   0.
    Image: svchost.exe

PROCESS ffff930ac18aa080
    SessionId: 0  Cid: 1284    Peb: 57b9d83000  ParentCid: 0274
    DirBase: 062fa002  ObjectTable: ffffcf8973622940  HandleCount: 218.
    Image: svchost.exe

PROCESS ffff930ac204e080
    SessionId: 0  Cid: 10ac    Peb: 5b6865c000  ParentCid: 0274
    DirBase: 11473d002  ObjectTable: ffffcf8974213b40  HandleCount: 444.
    Image: svchost.exe

PROCESS ffff930ac15240c0
    SessionId: 0  Cid: 10fc    Peb: 553075f000  ParentCid: 0274
    DirBase: 11ff89002  ObjectTable: ffffcf8974215a40  HandleCount: 486.
    Image: svchost.exe

PROCESS ffff930ac187f080
    SessionId: 0  Cid: 1210    Peb: 1ba19b3000  ParentCid: 0274
    DirBase: 199c7002  ObjectTable: ffffcf89742185c0  HandleCount: 89.
    Image: SgrmBroker.exe

PROCESS ffff930ac25f8240
    SessionId: 0  Cid: 1128    Peb: 7b8a3ec000  ParentCid: 0274
    DirBase: 1a334002  ObjectTable: ffffcf8974217a00  HandleCount: 386.
    Image: svchost.exe

PROCESS ffff930ac25ef300
    SessionId: 0  Cid: 0fc8    Peb: 620690000  ParentCid: 0274
    DirBase: 1a7f4002  ObjectTable: ffffcf8974217c40  HandleCount: 234.
    Image: svchost.exe

PROCESS ffff930ac16b5080
    SessionId: 0  Cid: 12ac    Peb: f296e0a000  ParentCid: 0274
    DirBase: 1a6ce002  ObjectTable: ffffcf897421a7c0  HandleCount: 663.
    Image: SearchIndexer.exe

PROCESS ffff930ac2761240
    SessionId: 0  Cid: 10d4    Peb: 694c8e8000  ParentCid: 0274
    DirBase: 1b8c7002  ObjectTable: ffffcf897361b480  HandleCount: 470.
    Image: svchost.exe

PROCESS ffff930ac27c2080
    SessionId: 0  Cid: 07f4    Peb: 677ece2000  ParentCid: 0274
    DirBase: 1cd7d002  ObjectTable: 00000000  HandleCount:   0.
    Image: svchost.exe

PROCESS ffff930ac29bb240
    SessionId: 0  Cid: 05bc    Peb: 70f52ad000  ParentCid: 0274
    DirBase: 22525002  ObjectTable: ffffcf8974f60480  HandleCount: 130.
    Image: svchost.exe

PROCESS ffff930ac2966080
    SessionId: 0  Cid: 08d0    Peb: b5533e1000  ParentCid: 0274
    DirBase: 2cbc2002  ObjectTable: ffffcf8974f660c0  HandleCount: 125.
    Image: svchost.exe

PROCESS ffff930ac29650c0
    SessionId: 0  Cid: 11b8    Peb: 9d4c77a000  ParentCid: 0274
    DirBase: 25c84002  ObjectTable: ffffcf8974f66a80  HandleCount: 227.
    Image: svchost.exe

PROCESS ffff930ac2bf6080
    SessionId: 0  Cid: 0834    Peb: 15d3714000  ParentCid: 0274
    DirBase: 3beb7002  ObjectTable: ffffcf89752d3e00  HandleCount: 252.
    Image: svchost.exe

PROCESS ffff930ac28ef080
    SessionId: 0  Cid: 0a34    Peb: db7ad52000  ParentCid: 0344
    DirBase: 3a9c6002  ObjectTable: ffffcf89752c8e80  HandleCount: 349.
    Image: usocoreworker.exe
```

```
PROCESS ffff930ac2b65080
    SessionId: 0  Cid: 07fc    Peb: 56538b5000  ParentCid: 0274
    DirBase: 11f332002  ObjectTable: ffffcf8973014500  HandleCount: 191.
    Image: svchost.exe

PROCESS ffff930ac54e02c0
    SessionId: 1  Cid: 13c0    Peb: cdab7e3000  ParentCid: 06a8
    DirBase: 70c84002  ObjectTable: ffffcf8977c65ac0  HandleCount: 639.
    Image: sihost.exe

PROCESS ffff930ac48e02c0
    SessionId: 1  Cid: 08c8    Peb: 11a5141000  ParentCid: 0274
    DirBase: 706ef002  ObjectTable: ffffcf8977c65dc0  HandleCount: 452.
    Image: svchost.exe

PROCESS ffff930ac2be3080
    SessionId: 1  Cid: 1088    Peb: e959ab6000  ParentCid: 0274
    DirBase: 72c08002  ObjectTable: ffffcf8979028180  HandleCount: 526.
    Image: svchost.exe

PROCESS ffff930ac42f3240
    SessionId: 0  Cid: 145c    Peb: b17d7b000  ParentCid: 0274
    DirBase: 7304b002  ObjectTable: ffffcf8977c68300  HandleCount: 155.
    Image: svchost.exe

PROCESS ffff930ac54c6080
    SessionId: 1  Cid: 14a0    Peb: aa9d677000  ParentCid: 0564
    DirBase: 738f0002  ObjectTable: ffffcf8979027800  HandleCount: 287.
    Image: taskhostw.exe

PROCESS ffff930ac51da240
    SessionId: 0  Cid: 14e0    Peb: a1cbeee000  ParentCid: 0274
    DirBase: 73ebb002  ObjectTable: ffffcf897618c0c0  HandleCount: 289.
    Image: svchost.exe

PROCESS ffff930ac57d7340
    SessionId: 1  Cid: 15c8    Peb: 1b0598e000  ParentCid: 0244
    DirBase: 74009002  ObjectTable: 00000000  HandleCount:   0.
    Image: userinit.exe

PROCESS ffff930ac57ec340
    SessionId: 1  Cid: 1600    Peb: 00b03000  ParentCid: 15c8
    DirBase: 7492b002  ObjectTable: ffffcf8977c68c80  HandleCount: 3104.
    Image: explorer.exe

PROCESS ffff930ac59e2300
    SessionId: 1  Cid: 16b8    Peb: 2a25f2f000  ParentCid: 0274
    DirBase: 751ac002  ObjectTable: ffffcf8977c69d80  HandleCount: 337.
    Image: svchost.exe

PROCESS ffff930ac58e8380
    SessionId: 1  Cid: 1728    Peb: b13df71000  ParentCid: 0344
    DirBase: 7a518002  ObjectTable: ffffcf897902ac00  HandleCount: 136.
    Image: dllhost.exe

PROCESS ffff930ac5b48080
    SessionId: 1  Cid: 17dc    Peb: 72e8cdc000  ParentCid: 0344
    DirBase: 7f25d002  ObjectTable: ffffcf8973616c40  HandleCount: 669.
    Image: StartMenuExperienceHost.exe

PROCESS ffff930ac5b9e300
    SessionId: 0  Cid: 1684    Peb: 876d26000  ParentCid: 0274
    DirBase: 7ff6a002  ObjectTable: ffffcf8979030540  HandleCount: 130.
    Image: svchost.exe

PROCESS ffff930ac5bdf300
    SessionId: 1  Cid: 175c    Peb: d5398c1000  ParentCid: 0344
    DirBase: 7f0b2002  ObjectTable: ffffcf8979030780  HandleCount: 323.
    Image: RuntimeBroker.exe

PROCESS ffff930ac5ba3080
    SessionId: 1  Cid: 185c    Peb: fe980f3000  ParentCid: 0344
    DirBase: 77483002  ObjectTable: ffffcf897618bc80  HandleCount: 1227.
    Image: SearchUI.exe

PROCESS ffff930ac5bee080
    SessionId: 1  Cid: 18c8    Peb: cf4822b000  ParentCid: 0344
```

```
        DirBase: 1a52d002  ObjectTable: ffffcf8979017a00  HandleCount: 592.
        Image: RuntimeBroker.exe

PROCESS ffff930ac5e20300
        SessionId: 1  Cid: 19cc    Peb: 6b6e38b000  ParentCid: 0344
        DirBase: 159bb002  ObjectTable: ffffcf8977c70a00  HandleCount: 363.
        Image: ApplicationFrameHost.exe

PROCESS ffff930ac5d79340
        SessionId: 1  Cid: 19d4    Peb: 6e599d0000  ParentCid: 0344
        DirBase: 101d7d002  ObjectTable: 00000000  HandleCount:   0.
        Image: MicrosoftEdge.exe

PROCESS ffff930ac5e660c0
        SessionId: 1  Cid: 1a50    Peb: 975f95b000  ParentCid: 0344
DeepFreeze
        DirBase: 0e734002  ObjectTable: ffffcf8979031100  HandleCount: 157.
        Image: SkypeBackgroundHost.exe

PROCESS ffff930ac5e69080
        SessionId: 1  Cid: 1ab8    Peb: 7dee61b000  ParentCid: 0344
DeepFreeze
        DirBase: 38909002  ObjectTable: ffffcf896ec28b00  HandleCount: 402.
        Image: YourPhone.exe

PROCESS ffff930ac5e95080
        SessionId: 1  Cid: 1b78    Peb: e891c2a000  ParentCid: 0344
        DirBase: 126f03002  ObjectTable: ffffcf896ec2a380  HandleCount: 300.
        Image: dllhost.exe

PROCESS ffff930ac5ee4080
        SessionId: 1  Cid: 1ba0    Peb: 3dc402c000  ParentCid: 0344
DeepFreeze
        DirBase: 3a37e002  ObjectTable: ffffcf897619b600  HandleCount: 437.
        Image: SkypeApp.exe

PROCESS ffff930ac5f3c0c0
        SessionId: 1  Cid: 1bf8    Peb: 6e6dfb5000  ParentCid: 0344
        DirBase: 1324ec002  ObjectTable: ffffcf897619be80  HandleCount: 344.
        Image: RuntimeBroker.exe

PROCESS ffff930abd155080
        SessionId: 1  Cid: 1ce8    Peb: 69f32db000  ParentCid: 0688
        DirBase: b0acc002  ObjectTable: ffffcf8977c72380  HandleCount: 432.
        Image: ctfmon.exe

PROCESS ffff930abd154080
        SessionId: 1  Cid: 1cf4    Peb: c9acff8000  ParentCid: 0688
        DirBase: b0a79002  ObjectTable: ffffcf8979034ec0  HandleCount: 314.
        Image: TabTip.exe

PROCESS ffff930ac2337080
        SessionId: 1  Cid: 1d6c    Peb: 66878a7000  ParentCid: 0344
        DirBase: 3904c002  ObjectTable: ffffcf8977c729c0  HandleCount: 305.
        Image: RuntimeBroker.exe

PROCESS ffff930ac2a960c0
        SessionId: 1  Cid: 1ecc    Peb: 20e7cc5000  ParentCid: 0344
        DirBase: acaf4002  ObjectTable: ffffcf897301a380  HandleCount: 224.
        Image: RuntimeBroker.exe

PROCESS ffff930ac28ed300
        SessionId: 1  Cid: 1f54    Peb: 8a41c49000  ParentCid: 0344
        DirBase: 11ea32002  ObjectTable: ffffcf8974f62780  HandleCount: 224.
        Image: RuntimeBroker.exe

PROCESS ffff930ac60a8080
        SessionId: 1  Cid: 09f8    Peb: bb5b4a5000  ParentCid: 0344
        DirBase: 3e5dc002  ObjectTable: ffffcf897c96ca00  HandleCount: 444.
        Image: smartscreen.exe

PROCESS ffff930ac53d4380
        SessionId: 1  Cid: 05c8    Peb: 351809f000  ParentCid: 1600
        DirBase: 7083f002  ObjectTable: ffffcf897c970380  HandleCount: 162.
        Image: SecurityHealthSystray.exe

PROCESS ffff930ac53d7080
        SessionId: 0  Cid: 02c0    Peb: 3f5e481000  ParentCid: 0274
```

```
        DirBase: 9bea3002  ObjectTable: ffffcf8977c5ab40  HandleCount: 406.
        Image: SecurityHealthService.exe

    PROCESS ffff930ac54d6080
        SessionId: 1  Cid: 0e4c    Peb: f3e5b5c000  ParentCid: 1600
        DirBase: af7ea002  ObjectTable: ffffcf8979008380  HandleCount: 544.
        Image: vmtoolsd.exe

    PROCESS ffff930ac53d6080
        SessionId: 1  Cid: 0e64    Peb: 00558000  ParentCid: 1600
        DirBase: 72c1c002  ObjectTable: ffffcf897c977c80  HandleCount: 637.
        Image: OneDrive.exe

    PROCESS ffff930ac2b62080
        SessionId: 0  Cid: 1c44    Peb: 4570ff4000  ParentCid: 0274
        DirBase: 12650a002  ObjectTable: ffffcf897c984cc0  HandleCount: 361.
        Image: svchost.exe

    PROCESS ffff930ac4237080
        SessionId: 0  Cid: 19b0    Peb: 9d6f5f9000  ParentCid: 0274
        DirBase: 12bea6002  ObjectTable: ffffcf8979017180  HandleCount: 155.
        Image: TrustedInstaller.exe

    PROCESS ffff930ac55de080
        SessionId: 1  Cid: 1ffc    Peb: 3c7ecc4000  ParentCid: 1600
        DirBase: 9c299002  ObjectTable: ffffcf897a68cd40  HandleCount: 141.
        Image: ApplicationA.exe

    PROCESS ffff930ac5f2d080
        SessionId: 1  Cid: 1dd0    Peb: 68b1074000  ParentCid: 1ffc
        DirBase: 64f34002  ObjectTable: ffffcf897a68d4c0  HandleCount: 206.
        Image: conhost.exe

    PROCESS ffff930ac26e1080
        SessionId: 0  Cid: 14dc    Peb: 2721b80000  ParentCid: 1158
        DirBase: 1215bb002  ObjectTable: ffffcf897a689c40  HandleCount: 325.
        Image: wuauclt.exe

    PROCESS ffff930ac6084080
        SessionId: 1  Cid: 0214    Peb: e27d4cf000  ParentCid: 1600
        DirBase: 5ad28002  ObjectTable: ffffcf89752ca940  HandleCount:  56.
        Image: ApplicationB.exe

    PROCESS ffff930ac62a3080
        SessionId: 1  Cid: 1f08    Peb: 4da3811000  ParentCid: 0214
        DirBase: 810f3002  ObjectTable: ffffcf89752cb800  HandleCount: 208.
        Image: conhost.exe

    PROCESS ffff930ac236e080
        SessionId: 1  Cid: 1da4    Peb: 5d75b3e000  ParentCid: 1600
        DirBase: 466b8002  ObjectTable: ffffcf897a6907c0  HandleCount:  56.
        Image: ApplicationC.exe

    PROCESS ffff930ac55e0400
        SessionId: 1  Cid: 1d54    Peb: 3d6410f000  ParentCid: 1da4
        DirBase: 8a30e002  ObjectTable: ffffcf897a68fd00  HandleCount: 208.
        Image: conhost.exe

    PROCESS ffff930ac63230c0
        SessionId: 1  Cid: 1df8    Peb: 00707000  ParentCid: 1600
        DirBase: 4f129002  ObjectTable: ffffcf8979019180  HandleCount:  52.
        Image: ApplicationD.exe

    PROCESS ffff930ac5eba300
        SessionId: 1  Cid: 1eac    Peb: 905ca2d000  ParentCid: 1df8
        DirBase: 8792d002  ObjectTable: ffffcf897901a040  HandleCount: 208.
        Image: conhost.exe

    PROCESS ffff930ac6262080
        SessionId: 0  Cid: 02a0    Peb: df1cbf1000  ParentCid: 0274
        DirBase: 8f3dc002  ObjectTable: ffffcf897c97e6c0  HandleCount: 135.
        Image: svchost.exe

    PROCESS ffff930ac5ea1080
        SessionId: 1  Cid: 1278    Peb: 00707000  ParentCid: 1df8
        DirBase: 84dd8002  ObjectTable: ffffcf897a695880  HandleCount:   0.
        Image: ApplicationD.exe
```

```
PROCESS ffff930ac61f7080
    SessionId: 1  Cid: 0bd8    Peb: d7ba05e000  ParentCid: 1df8
    DirBase: 3266f002  ObjectTable: ffffcf897a694340  HandleCount: 370.
    Image: WerFault.exe

PROCESS ffff930ac2be5080
    SessionId: 1  Cid: 0c58    Peb: 56ece5a000  ParentCid: 1600
    DirBase: 86166002  ObjectTable: ffffcf897a694bc0  HandleCount: 20055.
    Image: ApplicationE.exe

PROCESS ffff930ac629f080
    SessionId: 1  Cid: 1b90    Peb: d192663000  ParentCid: 0c58
    DirBase: 4df04002  ObjectTable: ffffcf897a697300  HandleCount: 208.
    Image: conhost.exe

PROCESS ffff930ac46e60c0
    SessionId: 0  Cid: 15904   Peb: 6eac584000  ParentCid: 0274
    DirBase: 11494b002  ObjectTable: ffffcf89752c8c80  HandleCount: 168.
    Image: VSSVC.exe

PROCESS ffff930ac5d78240
    SessionId: 0  Cid: 1593c   Peb: 57416d0000  ParentCid: 0274
    DirBase: 35177002  ObjectTable: ffffcf897a6890c0  HandleCount: 144.
    Image: svchost.exe

PROCESS ffff930acbf0b480
    SessionId: 0  Cid: 15984   Peb: e7e3b03000  ParentCid: 0344
    DirBase: 58dff002  ObjectTable: ffffcf897c96d3c0  HandleCount: 334.
    Image: TiWorker.exe

PROCESS ffff930ac2341080
    SessionId: 1  Cid: 159a8   Peb: 009fa000  ParentCid: 1600
    DirBase: 68ed6002  ObjectTable: ffffcf89752c7940  HandleCount: 159.
    Image: ApplicationA.exe

PROCESS ffff930ac2b640c0
    SessionId: 1  Cid: 159b0   Peb: 937e4d4000  ParentCid: 159a8
    DirBase: af317002  ObjectTable: ffffcf89752cac40  HandleCount: 208.
    Image: conhost.exe

PROCESS ffff930ac5dc4080
    SessionId: 1  Cid: 15a28   Peb: 7abcc79000  ParentCid: 0274
    DirBase: b4e7c002  ObjectTable: ffffcf897a68de40  HandleCount: 257.
    Image: svchost.exe

PROCESS ffff930ac6d5a080
    SessionId: 1  Cid: 158e8   Peb: 52c8f57000  ParentCid: 0344
DeepFreeze
    DirBase: 39092002  ObjectTable: ffffcf897841f8c0  HandleCount: 872.
    Image: MicrosoftEdge.exe

PROCESS ffff930ac5eec0c0
    SessionId: 1  Cid: 1290    Peb: 4a0c224000  ParentCid: 0344
    DirBase: 08efc002  ObjectTable: ffffcf8978421380  HandleCount: 393.
    Image: browser_broker.exe

PROCESS ffff930ac5ed4080
    SessionId: 1  Cid: 1fbc    Peb: f118f96000  ParentCid: 1bf8
DeepFreeze
    DirBase: 9fe3c002  ObjectTable: ffffcf8974f5ab40  HandleCount: 274.
    Image: MicrosoftEdgeSH.exe

PROCESS ffff930ac5e30080
    SessionId: 1  Cid: 06cc    Peb: f98446c000  ParentCid: 0344
DeepFreeze
    DirBase: b0625002  ObjectTable: ffffcf8974f5c900  HandleCount: 1039.
    Image: MicrosoftEdgeCP.exe

PROCESS ffff930ac629e080
    SessionId: 1  Cid: 158d0   Peb: f093939000  ParentCid: 0344
    DirBase: 40cbc002  ObjectTable: ffffcf897f29ac40  HandleCount: 569.
    Image: Microsoft.Photos.exe

PROCESS ffff930ac2b6a4c0
    SessionId: 1  Cid: 15b30   Peb: 747b1a8000  ParentCid: 0344
    DirBase: abb6f002  ObjectTable: ffffcf89801261c0  HandleCount: 507.
    Image: WindowsInternal.ComposableShell.Experiences.TextInput.InputApp.exe
```

```
PROCESS ffff930ac6286080
    SessionId: 0  Cid: 15cc    Peb: c2e827f000  ParentCid: 0274
    DirBase: 330f6002  ObjectTable: ffffcf8981a4ae40  HandleCount: 122.
    Image: svchost.exe

PROCESS ffff930ac6d66080
    SessionId: 1  Cid: 12f4    Peb: 9aa931000  ParentCid: 0344
DeepFreeze
    DirBase: 1368c3002  ObjectTable: ffffcf8981a4b6c0  HandleCount: 239.
    Image: backgroundTaskHost.exe

PROCESS ffff930ac46f52c0
    SessionId: 0  Cid: 15828   Peb: 8d687d000  ParentCid: 0970
    DirBase: 2e905002  ObjectTable: ffffcf8981a4c680  HandleCount: 177.
    Image: audiodg.exe

PROCESS ffff930ac6313240
    SessionId: 1  Cid: 15b40   Peb: 7116c54000  ParentCid: 0688
    DirBase: 34a47002  ObjectTable: 00000000  HandleCount:   0.
    Image: TabTip.exe

PROCESS ffff930ac63214c0
    SessionId: 1  Cid: 00b0    Peb: 456f822000  ParentCid: 1600
    DirBase: b1d6b002  ObjectTable: ffffcf8981a4be00  HandleCount:  75.
    Image: cmd.exe

PROCESS ffff930ac6260480
    SessionId: 1  Cid: 1bc0    Peb: d7113e7000  ParentCid: 00b0
    DirBase: 8ef8d002  ObjectTable: ffffcf8981a53940  HandleCount: 259.
    Image: conhost.exe

PROCESS ffff930ac58ec4c0
    SessionId: 1  Cid: 1e50    Peb: 9424076000  ParentCid: 0344
    DirBase: 138545002  ObjectTable: ffffcf898338cb40  HandleCount: 252.
    Image: RuntimeBroker.exe

PROCESS ffff930ac50df4c0
    SessionId: 1  Cid: 15ae4   Peb: ebacd37000  ParentCid: 00b0
    DirBase: 977e3002  ObjectTable: ffffcf898339be80  HandleCount: 123.
    Image: notmyfault64.exe
```

4. We notice *ApplicationE* process has an abnormally high number of handles. We thus identified **Handle Leak** pattern. We then look at the output of **!process 0 3f** command[1] and search for **Message Box** pattern (from a 64-bit process):

```
    THREAD ffff930ac49d0080  Cid 1ffc.109c  Teb: 0000003c7ecd1000 Win32Thread: ffff930ac62b44b0 WAIT:
(WrUserRequest) UserMode Non-Alertable
        ffff930ac621fc80  QueueObject
    Not impersonating
    DeviceMap                 ffffcf8978c103a0
    Owning Process            ffff930ac55de080    Image:        ApplicationA.exe
    Attached Process          N/A        Image:    N/A
    Wait Start TickCount      49071          Ticks: 976 (0:00:00:15.250)
    Context Switch Count      548            IdealProcessor: 1
    UserTime                  00:00:00.031
    KernelTime                00:00:00.015
    Win32 Start Address ApplicationA (0x00007ff64ed42c2c)
    Stack Init ffffef8637e84c90 Current ffffef8637e84490
    Base ffffef8637e85000 Limit ffffef8637e7f000 Call 0000000000000000
    Priority 10 BasePriority 8 PriorityDecrement 0 IoPriority 2 PagePriority 5
    Child-SP          RetAddr           Call Site
    ffffef86`37e844d0 fffff800`1151507d nt!KiSwapContext+0x76
    ffffef86`37e84610 fffff800`11513f04 nt!KiSwapThread+0xbfd
    ffffef86`37e846b0 fffff800`115136a5 nt!KiCommitThreadWait+0x144
    ffffef86`37e84750 fffff800`114dea6e nt!KeWaitForSingleObject+0x255
    ffffef86`37e84830 ffffdfa3`9b92962e nt!KeWaitForMultipleObjects+0x54e
    ffffef86`37e84940 ffffdfa3`9b929c55 win32kfull!xxxRealSleepThread+0x2be
    ffffef86`37e84a70 ffffdfa3`9b91c225 win32kfull!xxxSleepThread2+0xb5
    ffffef86`37e84ac0 fffff800`115d3c15 win32kfull!NtUserWaitMessage+0x65
    ffffef86`37e84b00 00007ffc`3fb71224 nt!KiSystemServiceCopyEnd+0x25 (TrapFrame @ ffffef86`37e84b00)
    0000003c`7f3ff748 00007ffc`4083bf90 win32u!NtUserWaitMessage+0x14
    0000003c`7f3ff750 00007ffc`4083bcff USER32!DialogBox2+0x260
    0000003c`7f3ff7f0 00007ffc`40882f99 USER32!InternalDialogBox+0x11b
```

---

[1] https://www.patterndiagnostics.com/files/fpma.txt

```
0000003c`7f3ff850 00007ffc`408819d5 USER32!SoftModalMessageBox+0x7e9
0000003c`7f3ff9a0 00007ffc`40882712 USER32!MessageBoxWorker+0x319
0000003c`7f3ffb50 00007ffc`4088279e USER32!MessageBoxTimeoutW+0x192
0000003c`7f3ffc50 00007ffc`3d2b23ff USER32!MessageBoxW+0x4e
0000003c`7f3ffc90 00007ff6`4ed41299 apphelp!MbHook_MessageBoxW+0x2f
0000003c`7f3ffce0 00007ff6`4ed42c89 ApplicationA+0x1299
0000003c`7f3ffd10 00007ffc`41937bd4 ApplicationA+0x2c89
0000003c`7f3ffd40 00007ffc`425cce51 KERNEL32!BaseThreadInitThunk+0x14
0000003c`7f3ffd70 00000000`00000000 ntdll!RtlUserThreadStart+0x21
```

5. We then look at the *fpma.txt* log again and search for one of **Wait Chain** pattern variants – for kernel synchronization object Mutant (Mutex):

```
THREAD ffff930ac2a850c0  Cid 1da4.0aa0  Teb: 0000005d75b4d000 Win32Thread: 0000000000000000 WAIT:
(UserRequest) UserMode Non-Alertable
        ffff930ac4f05ad0  Mutant - owning thread ffff930ac230f080
    Not impersonating
    DeviceMap                 ffffcf8978c103a0
    Owning Process            ffff930ac236e080       Image:         ApplicationC.exe
    Attached Process          N/A            Image:       N/A
    Wait Start TickCount      42255          Ticks: 7792 (0:00:02:01.750)
    Context Switch Count      6              IdealProcessor: 0
    UserTime                  00:00:00.000
    KernelTime                00:00:00.000
    Win32 Start Address ApplicationC (0x00007ff7b8f62ce0)
    Stack Init ffffef8637ebcc90 Current ffffef8637ebc6e0
    Base ffffef8637ebd000 Limit ffffef8637eb7000 Call 0000000000000000
    Priority 9 BasePriority 8 PriorityDecrement 0 IoPriority 2 PagePriority 5
    Child-SP          RetAddr           Call Site
    ffffef86`37ebc720 fffff800`1151507d nt!KiSwapContext+0x76
    ffffef86`37ebc860 fffff800`11513f04 nt!KiSwapThread+0xbfd
    ffffef86`37ebc900 fffff800`115136a5 nt!KiCommitThreadWait+0x144
    ffffef86`37ebc9a0 fffff800`11abd2bb nt!KeWaitForSingleObject+0x255
    ffffef86`37ebca80 fffff800`115d3c15 nt!NtWaitForSingleObject+0x10b
    ffffef86`37ebcb00 00007ffc`425fc0f4 nt!KiSystemServiceCopyEnd+0x25 (TrapFrame @ ffffef86`37ebcb00)
    0000005d`763ffdb8 00007ffc`3f8a8b03 ntdll!NtWaitForSingleObject+0x14
    0000005d`763ffdc0 00007ff7`b8f6136c KERNELBASE!WaitForSingleObjectEx+0x93
    0000005d`763ffe60 00007ff7`b8f62d3d ApplicationC+0x136c
    0000005d`763ffea0 00007ffc`41937bd4 ApplicationC+0x2d3d
    0000005d`763ffed0 00007ffc`425cce51 KERNEL32!BaseThreadInitThunk+0x14
    0000005d`763fff00 00000000`00000000 ntdll!RtlUserThreadStart+0x21
```

6. We see it is owned by a different thread, so we search for it in the *fpma.txt* log:

```
THREAD ffff930ac230f080  Cid 0214.12e4  Teb: 000000e27d4d6000 Win32Thread: 0000000000000000 WAIT:
(DelayExecution) UserMode Non-Alertable
        ffffffffffffffff  NotificationEvent
    Not impersonating
    DeviceMap                 ffffcf8978c103a0
    Owning Process            ffff930ac6084080       Image:         ApplicationB.exe
    Attached Process          N/A            Image:       N/A
    Wait Start TickCount      46238          Ticks: 3809 (0:00:00:59.515)
    Context Switch Count      6              IdealProcessor: 0
    UserTime                  00:00:00.000
    KernelTime                00:00:00.000
    Win32 Start Address ApplicationB (0x00007ff6887d2c2c)
    Stack Init ffffef8637f3ac90 Current ffffef8637f3a790
    Base ffffef8637f3b000 Limit ffffef8637f35000 Call 0000000000000000
    Priority 8 BasePriority 8 PriorityDecrement 0 IoPriority 2 PagePriority 5
    Child-SP          RetAddr           Call Site
    ffffef86`37f3a7d0 fffff800`1151507d nt!KiSwapContext+0x76
    ffffef86`37f3a910 fffff800`11513f04 nt!KiSwapThread+0xbfd
    ffffef86`37f3a9b0 fffff800`1150edb0 nt!KiCommitThreadWait+0x144
    ffffef86`37f3aa50 fffff800`11ab481f nt!KeDelayExecutionThread+0x4c0
    ffffef86`37f3aad0 fffff800`115d3c15 nt!NtDelayExecution+0x5f
    ffffef86`37f3ab00 00007ffc`425fc6f4 nt!KiSystemServiceCopyEnd+0x25 (TrapFrame @ ffffef86`37f3ab00)
    000000e2`7d8ffa28 00007ffc`3f8b6891 ntdll!NtDelayExecution+0x14
    000000e2`7d8ffa30 00007ff6`887d123f KERNELBASE!SleepEx+0xa1
    000000e2`7d8ffad0 00007ff6`887d2c89 ApplicationB+0x123f
    000000e2`7d8ffb00 00007ffc`41937bd4 ApplicationB+0x2c89
    000000e2`7d8ffb30 00007ffc`425cce51 KERNEL32!BaseThreadInitThunk+0x14
    000000e2`7d8ffb60 00000000`00000000 ntdll!RtlUserThreadStart+0x21
```

7. What we found is a wait chain from *ApplicationC* process thread to *ApplicationB* process thread. Alternatively, we could list the latter thread stack trace with appropriate flags to set its process context during the command execution:

```
0: kd> !thread ffff930ac230f080 1f
THREAD ffff930ac230f080  Cid 0214.12e4  Teb: 000000e27d4d6000 Win32Thread: 0000000000000000 WAIT:
(DelayExecution) UserMode Non-Alertable
    ffffffffffffffff  NotificationEvent
Not impersonating
DeviceMap                 ffffcf8978c103a0
Owning Process            ffff930ac6084080       Image:         ApplicationB.exe
Attached Process          N/A            Image:         N/A
Wait Start TickCount      46238          Ticks: 3809 (0:00:00:59.515)
Context Switch Count      6              IdealProcessor: 0
UserTime                  00:00:00.000
KernelTime                00:00:00.000
*** WARNING: Unable to verify checksum for ApplicationB.exe
Win32 Start Address ApplicationB (0x00007ff6887d2c2c)
Stack Init ffffef8637f3ac90 Current ffffef8637f3a790
Base ffffef8637f3b000 Limit ffffef8637f35000 Call 0000000000000000
Priority 8 BasePriority 8 PriorityDecrement 0 IoPriority 2 PagePriority 5
Child-SP          RetAddr           Call Site
ffffef86`37f3a7d0 fffff800`1151507d nt!KiSwapContext+0x76
ffffef86`37f3a910 fffff800`11513f04 nt!KiSwapThread+0xbfd
ffffef86`37f3a9b0 fffff800`1150edb0 nt!KiCommitThreadWait+0x144
ffffef86`37f3aa50 fffff800`11ab481f nt!KeDelayExecutionThread+0x4c0
ffffef86`37f3aad0 fffff800`115d3c15 nt!NtDelayExecution+0x5f
ffffef86`37f3ab00 00007ffc`425fc6f4 nt!KiSystemServiceCopyEnd+0x25 (TrapFrame @ ffffef86`37f3ab00)
000000e2`7d8ffa28 00007ffc`3f8b6891 ntdll!NtDelayExecution+0x14
000000e2`7d8ffa30 00007ff6`887d123f KERNELBASE!SleepEx+0xa1
000000e2`7d8ffad0 00007ff6`887d2c89 ApplicationB+0x123f
000000e2`7d8ffb00 00007ffc`41937bd4 ApplicationB+0x2c89
000000e2`7d8ffb30 00007ffc`425cce51 KERNEL32!BaseThreadInitThunk+0x14
000000e2`7d8ffb60 00000000`00000000 ntdll!RtlUserThreadStart+0x21
```

8. We now check for **Spiking Thread** pattern (the thread running on CPU 0 is a Task Manager thread we saw at step #1 above):

```
0: kd> !running

System Processors:  (0000000000000003)
  Idle Processors:  (0000000000000000)

     Prcbs              Current           (pri) Next            (pri) Idle
  0  fffff8000da14180   ffff930ac6077080  ( 9)                        fffff80011991400   ................
  1  ffff800149c56180   ffff930ac1cdd080  ( 9)                        fffff800149c670c0   ................

0: kd> !thread ffff930ac1cdd080 1f
THREAD ffff930ac1cdd080  Cid 15984.15a50  Teb: 000000e7e3b16000 Win32Thread: 0000000000000000 RUNNING on
processor 1
Impersonation token:  ffffcf897e131060 (Level Impersonation)
Owning Process            ffff930acbf0b480       Image:         TiWorker.exe
Attached Process          N/A            Image:         N/A
Wait Start TickCount      50047          Ticks: 0
Context Switch Count      74437          IdealProcessor: 0
UserTime                  00:00:14.859
KernelTime                00:00:23.390
Win32 Start Address cbscore!<lambda_4089d2f57d5829c9ce0855b1f31300ef>::<lambda_invoker_cdecl>
(0x00007ffc19eeb690)
Stack Init ffffef8652b87c90 Current ffffef8652b87980
Base ffffef8652b88000 Limit ffffef8652b82000 Call 0000000000000000
Priority 9 BasePriority 8 PriorityDecrement 0 IoPriority 2 PagePriority 5
Child-SP          RetAddr           Call Site
000000e7`e3ffc9f0 00007ffc`3f7a58ed bcryptPrimitives!SymCryptSha256AppendBlocks_ul1+0xa44
000000e7`e3ffcbc0 00007ffc`3f7a5748 bcryptPrimitives!SymCryptSha256Append+0x4d
000000e7`e3ffcc00 00007ffc`3fb234a7 bcryptPrimitives!MSCryptHashData+0xf8
000000e7`e3ffcca0 00007ffc`19aee831 bcrypt!BCryptHashData+0x77
000000e7`e3ffccf0 00007ffc`19aee0ac wcp!RtlHashLBlob+0xa1
000000e7`e3ffcd60 00007ffc`19aec19c wcp!ComponentStore::CRawStoreLayout::FetchManifestContent+0x3cc
000000e7`e3ffd120 00007ffc`19aebe76 wcp!ComponentStore::CRawStoreLayout::FetchManifest+0x130
000000e7`e3ffd380 00007ffc`19a97c72 wcp!ComponentStore::CRawStoreLayout::FetchManifest+0x2ca
000000e7`e3ffd510 00007ffc`19d00506 wcp!
ComponentStore::CRawStoreLayout::TriggerPopulationOfComponentVersionedIndexKey+0xda
000000e7`e3ffd650 00007ffc`19a7f773 wcp!ComponentStore::CRawStoreLayout::QueryComponentProperties+0x23e126
```

```
000000e7`e3ffd790 00007ffc`19a7eb44 wcp!ComponentStore::CRawStoreLayout::AnalyzeComponentForScavenge+0x34b
000000e7`e3ffda90 00007ffc`19bb9d09 wcp!ComponentStore::CRawStoreLayout::PlanComponentStoreScavenge+0x320
000000e7`e3ffdf20 00007ffc`19bbd365 wcp!ComponentStore::CRawStoreLayout::Scavenge+0x2c9
000000e7`e3ffe240 00007ffc`19b40435 wcp!CCSIDirectTransaction::Scavenge+0x385
000000e7`e3ffe380 00007ffc`19b400de wcp!CCSIDirectTransaction::Operate+0x325
000000e7`e3ffe620 00007ffc`19a9b095 wcp!CCSIDirectTransaction_IRtlTransaction::Operate+0x12e
000000e7`e3ffe6c0 00007ffc`19a998ea wcp!Windows::COM::CComponentStore::InternalTransact+0x177d
000000e7`e3ffeee0 00007ffc`19ccbd43 wcp!Windows::COM::CComponentStore_IStore::Transact2+0x4a
000000e7`e3ffef40 00007ffc`19cce925 wcp!
Windows::ServicingAPI::CCSITransaction::GeneratePendingTransactionContent+0x27f
000000e7`e3fff060 00007ffc`19cd6b4c wcp!Windows::ServicingAPI::CCSITransaction::ICSITransaction_Commit+0x2ad
000000e7`e3fff380 00007ffc`19e5681d wcp!Windows::ServicingAPI::CCSITransaction_ICSITransaction::Commit+0x12c
000000e7`e3fff590 00007ffc`19ecf2a2 cbscore!TransactionCommit+0x65
000000e7`e3fff5d0 00007ffc`19f11a06 cbscore!PackageStoreCsiScavenge+0x24e
000000e7`e3fff6b0 00007ffc`19f0f2d7 cbscore!CCbsMaintenanceExecutionObject::Scavenge+0x186
000000e7`e3fff740 00007ffc`19e609b7 cbscore!CCbsMaintenanceExecutionObject::Execute+0x867
000000e7`e3fff870 00007ffc`41937bd4 cbscore!ExecutionEngineSchedule+0x73
000000e7`e3fff8a0 00007ffc`425cce51 KERNEL32!BaseThreadInitThunk+0x14
000000e7`e3fff8d0 00000000`00000000 ntdll!RtlUserThreadStart+0x21
```

8. We see that the thread running on CPU 1 consumed some time in both user and kernel modes. Since the system appears busy (all CPUs are active), we also check for Ready threads.

```
0: kd> !ready
KSHARED_READY_QUEUE fffff8000da1a700: (00) **------------------------------------------------------------
SharedReadyQueue fffff8000da1a700: Ready Threads at priority 8
    THREAD ffff930ac224b080  Cid 0c14.0418  Teb: 000000ade0765000 Win32Thread: ffff930ac254b7a0 READY on
processor 80000001
    THREAD ffff930ac5dc3080  Cid 0c58.1af8  Teb: 00000056ece5b000 Win32Thread: 0000000000000000 READY on
processor 80000000
    THREAD ffff930abd933040  Cid 0004.00ec  Teb: 0000000000000000 Win32Thread: 0000000000000000 READY on
processor 80000001
    THREAD ffff930ac1de4080  Cid 0c14.0d3c  Teb: 000000ade0755000 Win32Thread: 0000000000000000 READY on
processor 80000000
SharedReadyQueue fffff8000da1a700: Ready Threads at priority 5
    THREAD ffff930ac1e36040  Cid 0bf8.0d68  Teb: 000000ce7c002000 Win32Thread: ffff930ac21f2bf0 READY on
processor 80000000
SharedReadyQueue fffff8000da1a700: Ready Threads at priority 4
    THREAD ffff930ac1b40080  Cid 081c.0ba4  Teb: 0000000000000000 Win32Thread: 0000000000000000 READY on
processor 80000000
SharedReadyQueue fffff8000da1a700: Ready Threads at priority 0
    THREAD ffff930abcfac080  Cid 0004.0038  Teb: 0000000000000000 Win32Thread: 0000000000000000 READY on
processor 80000001
Processor 0: No threads in READY state
Processor 1: Group Scheduling Queue

    Scb: ffff930ac28a0778 Rank: 2 OQHistory: 0000000000015555
    GenCycles: 706070 LTCycles: 21604816, MinTarget: 633600000, MaxTarget: 1267200000, RankTarget: 63360000
    nt!_KSCB ffff930ac28a0778: Ready Threads at priority 9
        THREAD ffff930ac62c70c0  Cid 158d0.14a8  Teb: 000000f09395c000 Win32Thread: 0000000000000000 READY
on processor 1
```

9. We check all threads in the log and find one that belongs to *ApplicationE* which seems was **Active Thread**, doing some math calculations, and then interrupted:

```
        THREAD ffff930ac5dc3080  Cid 0c58.1af8  Teb: 00000056ece5b000 Win32Thread: 0000000000000000 READY on
processor 80000000
        Not impersonating
        DeviceMap                 ffffcf8978c103a0
        Owning Process            ffff930ac2be5080     Image:          ApplicationE.exe
        Attached Process          N/A          Image:      N/A
        Wait Start TickCount      50046        Ticks: 1 (0:00:00:00.015)
        Context Switch Count      131578       IdealProcessor: 1
        UserTime                  00:01:14.640
        KernelTime                00:00:00.187
*** WARNING: Unable to verify checksum for ApplicationE.exe
        Win32 Start Address ApplicationE!wmainCRTStartup (0x00007ff651191670)
        Stack Init ffffef86375bbc90 Current ffffef86375bb970
        Base ffffef86375bc000 Limit ffffef86375b6000 Call 0000000000000000
        Priority 8 BasePriority 8 PriorityDecrement 0 IoPriority 2 PagePriority 5
        Child-SP          RetAddr           Call Site
        ffffef86`375bb9b0 fffff800`115c8a35 nt!KxDispatchInterrupt+0x144
        ffffef86`375bbaf0 fffff800`115c3ee1 nt!KiDpcInterruptBypass+0x25
        ffffef86`375bbb00 00007ff6`51192f7a nt!KiInterruptDispatch+0xb1 (TrapFrame @ ffffef86`375bbb00)
```

```
        00000056`ecd2f840 00007ff6`511913e7 ApplicationE!sqrt+0xc2 [d:\th\minkernel\crts\ucrt\src\appcrt\
tran\noti386\sqrt.c @ 74]
        00000056`ecd2f8a0 00007ff6`5119160c ApplicationE!wmain+0x87 [c:\awmda-examples\applicatione\
applicatione\applicatione.cpp @ 79]
        (Inline Function) --------`-------- ApplicationE!invoke_main+0x22 (Inline Function @
00007ff6`5119160c) [f:\dd\vctools\crt\vcstartup\src\startup\exe_common.inl @ 79]
        00000056`ecd2f8d0 00007ffc`41937bd4 ApplicationE!__scrt_common_main_seh+0x124 [f:\dd\vctools\crt\
vcstartup\src\startup\exe_common.inl @ 255]
        00000056`ecd2f910 00007ffc`425cce51 KERNEL32!BaseThreadInitThunk+0x14
        00000056`ecd2f940 00000000`00000000 ntdll!RtlUserThreadStart+0x21
```

10. Then we also check for patterns in the combined x86 and x64 script output log[2] and find another instance of **Message Box** pattern (now from a 32-bit process):

```
THREAD ffff930ac5e15080  Cid 159a8.159e4  Teb: 000000000080c000 Win32Thread: ffff930ac912ee50 WAIT: (WrUserRequest) UserMode Non-Alertable
    ffff930ac6137a00  QueueObject
Not impersonating
DeviceMap                 ffffcf8978c103a0
Owning Process            ffff930ac2341080     Image:         ApplicationA.exe
Attached Process          N/A          Image:         N/A
Wait Start TickCount      49071        Ticks: 976 (0:00:00:15.250)
Context Switch Count      418          IdealProcessor: 0
UserTime                  00:00:00.000
KernelTime                00:00:00.031
*** WARNING: Unable to verify checksum for ApplicationA.exe
Win32 Start Address ApplicationA (0x00000000006b2ac7)
Stack Init ffffef8636d33c90 Current ffffef8636d33490
Base ffffef8636d34000 Limit ffffef8636d2e000 Call 0000000000000000
Priority 10 BasePriority 8 PriorityDecrement 0 IoPriority 2 PagePriority 5
Child-SP          RetAddr           : Args to Child                                                           : Call Site
ffffef86`36d334d0 fffff800`1151507d : ffff8001`00000001 0000000a`0000000a ffff930a`ffffffff 00000000`00000002 : nt!KiSwapContext+0x76
ffffef86`36d33610 fffff800`11513f04 : ffff930a`c5e15080 fffff800`0da14180 ffff930a`c50d61f0 fffff800`00000000 : nt!KiSwapThread+0xbfd
ffffef86`36d336b0 fffff800`115136a5 : ffff930a`c0036b90 00000000`00000000 00000000`00000000 00000000`00000000 : nt!KiCommitThreadWait+0x144
ffffef86`36d33750 fffff800`114dea6e : ffff930a`c6137a00 00000000`0000000d 00000000`00000901 00000000`00017c00 : nt!KeWaitForSingleObject+0x255
ffffef86`36d33830 fffdfa3`9b92962e : fffdfd2`8388d8a0 fffdfd2`8388d8a0 00000000`00000000 00000000`00000000 : nt!KeWaitForMultipleObjects+0x54e
ffffef86`36d33940 fffdfa3`9b929c55 : 00000000`77dd3620 00000000`00000000 00000000`00000000  fffff780`00000000 : win32kfull!
xxxRealSleepThread+0x2be
ffffef86`36d33a70 fffdfa3`9b91c225 : ffffef86`36d33b80 00000000`028efabc 00000000`77dd3620 00000000`00000001 : win32kfull!xxxSleepThread2+0xb5
ffffef86`36d33ac0 fffff800`115d3c15 : ffff930a`c5e15000 ffff930a`c5e15080 00000000`0080c000 00000000`00000113 : win32kfull!NtUserWaitMessage+0x65
ffffef86`36d33b00 00000000`77dd1cbc : 00000000`77dd1c7b 00000023`778e2bac 00000000`00000023 00000000`028efacc : nt!KiSystemServiceCopyEnd+0x25
(TrapFrame @ ffffef86`36d33b00)
00000000`024ceed8 00000000`77dd1c7b : 00000023`778e2bac 00000000`00000023 00000000`028efacc 00000000`028efa18 : wow64cpu!CpupSyscallStub+0xc
00000000`024ceee0 00000000`77dd1199 : 00000000`028efc44 00007ffc`4214c864 00000000`024cefb0 00007ffc`4214bf58 : wow64cpu!Thunk0Arg+0x5
00000000`024cef90 00007ffc`4214c77a : 00000000`00b7b6f0 00000000`006b0110 00000000`00000000 00000000`024cf3d0 : wow64cpu!BTCpuSimulate+0x9
00000000`024cefd0 00007ffc`4214c637 : 00000000`00000000 00000000`00000001 00000000`00000000 00000000`00000000 : wow64!RunCpuSimulation+0xa
00000000`024cf000 00007ffc`425d18eb : 00000000`00000000 00000000`00000000 00000000`00000001 00000000`00000000 : wow64!Wow64LdrpInitialize+0x127
00000000`024cf2b0 00007ffc`425d17d3 : 00000000`00000000 00007ffc`42560000 00000000`0080c000 00000000`00000000 : ntdll!_LdrpInitialize+0xff
00000000`024cf350 00007ffc`425d177e : 00000000`024cf3d0 00000000`00000000 00000000`00000000 00000000`00000000 : ntdll!LdrpInitialize+0x3b
00000000`024cf380 00000000`00000000 : 00000000`00000000 00000000`00000000 00000000`00000000 00000000`00000000 : ntdll!LdrInitializeThunk+0xe


.process /p /r 0
Implicit thread is now ffff930a`c5e15080
WARNING: WOW context retrieval requires
switching to the thread's process context.
Use .process /p ffff930a`c50df4c0 to switch back.
Implicit process is now ffff930a`c2341080
x86 context set
Loading Kernel Symbols
...............................................................Page 200003190 too large to be in the dump file.
.
......................................................................
......................................................
....
Loading User Symbols
.....
Loading unloaded module list
.......
Loading Wow64 Symbols
..............................
 # ChildEBP         RetAddr           Args to Child
00 028efab8 756ab3c3 00000000 00000000 00000000 win32u!NtUserWaitMessage+0xc (FPO: [0,0,0])
01 028efaf8 756ab2b4 00000000 00000000 756f0010 USER32!DialogBox2+0x102 (FPO: [Non-Fpo])
02 028efb28 756f1acb 00000000 756f0010 028efd68 USER32!InternalDialogBox+0xd9 (FPO: [Non-Fpo])
03 028efbf4 756f0967 028efd68 006bd18c 00000000 USER32!SoftModalMessageBox+0x72b (FPO: [1,41,4])
04 028efd50 756f1345 00000000 756f1370 00b7b6f0 USER32!MessageBoxWorker+0x2ca (FPO: [Non-Fpo])
05 028efdd8 756f138a 00000000 006bd18c 006bd180 USER32!MessageBoxTimeoutW+0x165 (FPO: [6,29,4])
06 028efdf8 6fcc3ddb 00000000 006bd18c 006bd180 USER32!MessageBoxW+0x1a (FPO: [Non-Fpo])
*** WARNING: Unable to verify checksum for ApplicationA.exe
07 028efe3c 006b12e0 00000000 006bd18c 006bd180 apphelp!MbHook_MessageBoxW+0x2b (FPO: [Non-Fpo])
WARNING: Stack unwind information not available. Following frames may be wrong.
08 028efe54 006b2b1e 00000000 5e297847 006b2ac7 ApplicationA+0x12e0
09 028efe90 772c6359 00b7b6f0 772c6340 028efefc ApplicationA+0x2b1e
0a 028efea4 77e47c14 00b7b6f0 cc8cd7d4 00000000 KERNEL32!BaseThreadInitThunk+0x19 (FPO: [Non-Fpo])
0b 028efefc 77e47be4 ffffffff 77e68feb 00000000 ntdll_77de0000!__RtlUserThreadStart+0x2f (FPO: [SEH])
0c 028eff0c 00000000 006b2ac7 00b7b6f0 00000000 ntdll_77de0000!_RtlUserThreadStart+0x1b (FPO: [Non-Fpo])
```

---

[2] https://www.patterndiagnostics.com/files/fpma-full.txt

Agenda (Guide)

- Patterns related to complete memory dumps

- Pattern cooperation case studies from complete memory dumps

- Pattern Map

© 2020 Software Diagnostics Services

Now I show you a few pattern names and their description links. Since the second version, the pattern descriptions and case studies are only available for users of the Software Diagnostics Library, in Memory Dump Analysis Anthology volumes, or Encyclopedia of Crash Dump Analysis Patterns.

Pattern Examples

Some basic analysis patterns that are relevant to complete memory dumps:

Incorrect Symbolic Information	No System Dumps
Semantic Split	Message Box
Paged Out Data	Inconsistent Dump
Wait Chain (thread objects)	Wait Chain (critical sections)
Wait Chain (LPC/ALPC)	Wait Chain (process objects)
Last Error Collection	Special Process
Suspended Thread	Historical Information
Coupled Processes (strong)	Stack Trace Collection
Truncated Dump	Insufficient Memory (handle leak)
Spiking Thread	Main Thread
Deadlock (critical sections)	Suspended Thread
Problem Vocabulary	Pleiades
Semantic Structures	Dual Stack Trace
Virtualized System	

There are many more analysis patterns. Here I only list a few. All of them can be found on the Software Diagnostics Institute website and its Software Diagnostics Library: www.DumpAnalysis.org.

Case Studies

17 pattern interaction case studies using complete memory dumps:

http://www.dumpanalysis.org/blog/index.php/category/complete-memory-dump-analysis/

Each case study includes several patterns and is useful to see how analysis patterns are used, and problem patterns are diagnosed in context. The content is available for users of Software Diagnostics Library and in Memory Dump Analysis Anthology volumes:

https://www.dumpanalysis.org/blog/index.php/category/complete-memory-dump-analysis/

WinDbg Command Map

Pattern <-> WinDbg command

WinDbg command map is a handy table compiled from pattern examples. It shows which WinDbg commands can be used for memory dump inspection if you suspect a particular pattern. Unfortunately, hundreds of new patterns have been added since the publication of this map, so it needs a revision now.

Pattern <-> WinDbg command:

https://www.amazon.com/Dmitry-Vostokov-ebook/dp/B01034WL9U/

Reference Resources

- WinDbg Help / WinDbg.org (quick links)
- DumpAnalysis.org / SoftwareDiagnostics.Institute / PatternDiagnostics.com
- Debugging.TV / YouTube.com/DebuggingTV / YouTube.com/PatternDiagnostics
- Encyclopedia of Crash Dump Analysis Patterns, 2nd edition
- Memory Dump Analysis Anthology (Volume 13 is forthcoming in 2020)

Some useful resources. WinDbg.org also contains links to various WinDbg-related books written by other authors and me.

WinDbg quick links
http://WinDbg.org

Software Diagnostics Institute
https://www.dumpanalysis.org

Debugging.TV
http://debugging.tv

Pattern Diagnostics Seminars
https://www.youtube.com/PatternDiagnostics

Software Diagnostics Services
https://www.patterndiagnostics.com

Encyclopedia of Crash Dump Analysis Patterns, 2nd edition
https://www.dumpanalysis.org/encyclopedia-crash-dump-analysis-patterns

Memory Dump Analysis Anthology
https://www.dumpanalysis.org/advanced-software-debugging-reference

Since the third version of this seminar, the new editions of training courses that use physical memory analysis have been added.

Accelerated Windows Memory Dump Analysis, 4th + 5th editions:
https://www.patterndiagnostics.com/accelerated-windows-memory-dump-analysis-book

Advanced Windows Memory Dump Analysis with Data Structures, 3rd edition
https://www.patterndiagnostics.com/advanced-windows-memory-dump-analysis-book

Accelerated Windows Malware Analysis with Memory Dumps, 2nd edition
https://www.patterndiagnostics.com/accelerated-windows-malware-analysis-book

Accelerated Windows Debugging[3], 2nd edition
https://www.patterndiagnostics.com/accelerated-windows-debugging-book